BENNO

BENNO
My Life in Football

DAVE BENNETT
with Rich Chamberlain

First published by Pitch Publishing, 2024

Pitch Publishing
9 Donnington Park,
85 Birdham Road,
Chichester, West Sussex,
PO20 7AJ
www.pitchpublishing.co.uk
info@pitchpublishing.co.uk

© 2024, Dave Bennett with Rich Chamberlain

Every effort has been made to trace the copyright.
Any oversight will be rectified in future editions at the
earliest opportunity by the publisher.

All rights reserved. No part of this book may be reproduced,
sold or utilised in any form or transmitted in any form or by
any means, electronic or mechanical, including photocopying,
recording or by any information storage and retrieval system,
without prior permission in writing from the publisher.

A CIP catalogue record is available for this book
from the British Library.

ISBN 978 1 80150 750 9

Printed and bound in the UK on FSC® certified paper in line
with our continuing commitment to ethical business practices,
sustainability and the environment.

Typesetting and origination by Pitch Publishing

Printed and bound by TJ Books, UK

Contents

Acknowledgements 7

Foreword: John Sillett 9

Prologue: Baptism of Fire. 13

1. The Early Years: Hometown Hero 17
2. On My Way to Wembley. 37
3. Off to the Valleys. 64
4. Sky-High Blues 96
5. History Repeating 120
6. The Hat-Trick of Great Escapes 144
7. A New Era 161
8. Here We Go 181
9. Shopping in Harrods. 205
10. From Wembley to Wednesday. 227
11. The End is Nigh 240

Acknowledgements

I WOULD like to say a big thank you to all my scouts, coaches, playing colleagues, my managers, my friends and family for backing me and making my dream come true. Thank you for giving me the opportunity to play the game I love, football.

Dave Bennett
July, 2024

Foreword: John Sillett

HE WAS a class act, Dave, a confident fella, smart, well-dressed, he was always bouncy, laughing, trying to get one over on you. You knew Dave was around, whether at the Sky Blue Connexion, the dressing room, out and about, he had a great presence. He mixed well, when you needed to turn the tap on, he knew how to do it! He was a player who you could demonstrate through him as the right example to other players, this is what you ought to be aspiring to. He had so much skill, good pace, a great body swerve and was a great crosser of the ball. You put those elements together and you've got some player. For me, he was a marvellous outlet in as much as he could destroy most of the full-backs he came up against. He had that ability to play out wide or you could play him up front with Cyrille Regis; they combined well as a strike pair and gave us good movement off the ball. His strength for me was always on the right wing. I never had to look for anybody else to fill that role; when you're picking a team, his name would be in there in the No.7 shirt. The great cross I'll always remember is, of course, from the cup final. It was a brilliant cross, so accurate; it's one of those moves that you always remember. It had good pace but just enough to take it away from Ray Clemence and behind Richard Gough and Gary Mabbutt.

Dave was always the life and soul of the dressing room. He'd always have a laugh at what was going on, whether it was the players talking or me and George giving out the instructions. He always supported me and had great ability to win a game for us with one piece of magic. Out of nothing he could change a game and we often benefitted from this. As a player, he backed me to the hilt, and you can't ask for any more as a manager.

When I stepped up from youth coach to first-team coach in April 1986, it was one of those moves where you wondered yourself if it was going to work. The boys had watched my youth team and said why can't we play like that; they'd played a long-ball game under Don Mackay. John Poynton, our chairman at the time, watched our youth team and saw how well we played and said he liked what he'd watched and put George and me in charge of the first team. We changed the playing style overnight and the transformation was clear for all to see. The ball was played in to Cyrille's feet, his strength, and we built the play around him. Nobody could knock him off the ball, he was so strong, such a great player with so many attributes. I lost count of the number of times he'd hold off the defender and lay it out wide to Benno, hugging the touchline. Teams found it hard to contain us and we became entertainers overnight. They were a great pair, worked well together; the spell when they played up front together worked very well.

To bounce back from not one but four broken legs shows the amazing character of the man; you couldn't knock him down, he always bounced back and proved any doubters wrong. I'd say to him that he was up front today with Cyrille, to which he'd reply, 'You want to see genius again then, Sill!' He was never short of confidence. It's great to work with players who are always laughing and enjoying their work.

Dave played under so many top managers in his career – Malcolm Allison, John Bond, Len Ashurst, Big Ron, Ossie Ardiles and Glenn Hoddle – it's a tribute to his ability. He's a player worth reading about, never a dull moment. He gave so much to Coventry City in my time there and was never a problem throughout my time with him. I knew I could rely on him, he's just that type of person.

Prologue

Baptism of Fire

MAINE ROAD, 14 April 1979. With 75 minutes on the clock, Roy Bailey raises the No.4 board for Tommy Booth to leave the pitch.

There are 40,000 fans in the famous old ground. I'm wearing the No.12 shirt and stand quietly while I wait for Tommy to shake my hand. The atmosphere around me is crackling, as it always is, and Tony Book wishes me well as I prepare to cross the white line. It's three months before my 20th birthday and I'm about to make my first-team debut for Manchester City. On the pitch, looking over in my direction, are the likes of Joe Corrigan, Dave Watson, Paul Power, Tony Henry, Asa Hartford and Peter Barnes. I've earned their trust and respect in the many hours spent on the training ground and in Central League matches; now it's time for me to step up and show them, my family and the support just what I can do in a City shirt.

Everton will go on to finish the season in fourth and qualify for the UEFA Cup. I go on, feeling sharp, bright, ten feet tall. Within minutes I pick up the ball and move into the Everton half. As I step past one of their players he brings me crashing to the floor. As I fall to the turf, he picks me up and whispers, 'Do that again, you black bastard, I'll break your leg.' I go from a size nine to a size two at that point. You think to yourself, *Is this what it's all about?*

You've got to man up and deal with it there and then. I'd had a bit of abuse in the reserves but all I was worried about when I got back in the dressing room was: *Did I do alright?* I didn't have a mentor to seek out, there was no ear for me to vent. The only other black guy playing there at the time was Roger Palmer. I had nowhere to turn. I had to deal with it my way then take it on and find out the rights and wrongs.

They were looking at how you looked after yourself, and your temperament. I was learning all the time. Being a black guy and a local lad, they were really looking closely. It was very difficult. I was cleaning my own boots. After I got the year's contract I was still only a young kid, and with all of the racism I didn't need to be good, I needed to be excellent. Playing in those reserve fixtures didn't just test my ability, it was testing my character too. The lads at Man

City always looked out for me. There was no animosity from them. They thought my character was alright, hence the club took me on, but I still had to look out for myself because players wanted to kick you. Playing in that reserve league against all the older pros made me grow up a lot quicker. It was playing against men. You knew you were going to get tackled. I was taught how to look after myself, how to tackle, how to foul.

There was a cliché about black players not liking to play in the cold. We had to clear that out. It was always frosty back then and we had lots of snow. We had to play in all types of weather. There were only a few black guys in the top division; it was me and the three guys from West Brom. Coming through as a black player at that time was a massive thing to undertake. Some of those crowds at Man City, as you can imagine, they were unforgiving.

I grew up with racism around me. It was everywhere. I had to look after myself in more ways than one in life because I lived in the ghetto of Manchester. We had skinheads, greasers, all kinds of groups. I knew about all of that and I'd been told to look after myself, but it was still a shock to the system when you have a pro saying that to you on the pitch. When that happens, reality sets in and you think about what you're going to do. If I ever saw him now I don't know if I'd shake his hand to say thanks for that because it woke me up, or punch him in the mouth and say, 'Now what're you gonna say?' Growing up I had to face that kind of abuse and at that very moment I realised what I had to do to succeed on the pitch. I had to be smart and grow up fast. And I did.

1
The Early Years: Hometown Hero

LONGSIGHT, THREE miles south of Manchester city centre, is an inner-city area flanked by Ardwick and West Gorton to the north, Belle Vue to the east, Levenshulme to the south and Chorlton-on-Medlock, Victoria Park and Fallowfield to the west. Around 15,000 people live there and, to the Bennett family, it was home.

We lived within walking distance of Maine Road. My mum Lucy and dad Zeddy brought up Gary and me. Gary was born in December 1961. I was 18 months older, born in July 1959. Longsight was a tough place to be brought up. I went to St John's Primary School and then on to Burnage Grammar. To go to the grammar school in those days you had to be selected, and it was an all-boys' establishment. I learned how to play cricket and rugby alongside my football, and it was a good education all round for me. My athletics wasn't too bad either, but the round ball was my focus, even though I didn't think I was going to get anywhere with it. I simply enjoyed playing the game.

Racism was always there, but going to an all-boys' school I didn't see much. However, in youth clubs and similar there were always fights with skinheads and punks. Unfortunately, you were always going to get that growing up where I did. You had to know how to look after yourself, as there was always an undercurrent, whether on your doorstep or in your face, so you'd have to look out for yourself, otherwise you'd get beaten up and bullied every day.

At Burnage Grammar one of my team-mates was Peter Coyne. Peter played for England Schoolboys and scored successive hat-tricks against France and West Germany in 1974. Manchester United signed him and he left school in the Easter holidays of our last year. It all depended on your birthday, and with him being one of the eldest he was able to go. Peter was all the rage locally and nationally; England beat France 5-2 and West Germany 4-0, and he was headline news. Schoolboy internationals drew huge crowds as schools across the country were given tickets to bring coachloads of pupils, often watching at Wembley for the first time, while the matches were also televised on ITV. Peter was top scorer for United's reserves and made his first-team debut at Villa Park, aged 17, in February 1976. It was United's first season back in the First Division after their ignominious relegation in 1973/74. The penultimate match of the season at Leicester saw Tommy Docherty start Coyne, and he responded with a goal in a 2-1 defeat. United finished the season in third, yet Peter never made another first-team appearance. Disciplinary problems saw his contract cancelled within a year as Docherty released him and he initially drifted into non-league circles. Our paths, however, would very nearly cross again in years to come.

While Peter was over at Old Trafford, I was playing for Ashwood Celtic, and our rivals at the time were a team called Senrab, who were formed by the notorious Barry Bennell. We knew all their players as we'd been teammates for Manchester Boys in earlier seasons. While I was at Ashwood, a local Arabian side, Adenor, asked me to play for them on Saturdays and Sundays. The football was of a high standard and soon I was getting rave reviews. Adenor sent me for a trial at Oldham, and while I was there a scout by the name of Len Davies noticed me and asked me to go to Manchester City for trials and training. My brother Gary played for Senrab a couple of years below me, along with Moss Side youth club. In his side were Clive Wilson, Alex Williams, Steve Kinsey and Andy May.

We played Blackpool in the Lancashire Cup at Maine Road, won 5-1, and I scored a hat-trick. The brief was that if I did well they'd keep me, but if I struggled, I'd be shown the door. I started playing in the A team and B team and was offered a year's contract to play in the youth team. I by-passed having to carry out apprentice duties due to the date I joined with my July birthday, this being the spring of 1976. I was 16, 17 in the July, and trained initially while I was at college and then they asked me to play on Saturdays for the youth team. On 26 November 1976, I signed my first professional contract. Club secretary Bernard Halford helped me with the contract, which ran until the end of June 1977. I earned £35 per week. It had its bonuses, of course, an additional £5 per week if I played in the Central League, and up to £10 in the first team. The contract also had an option for a further year to take me up to the summer of 1978 and would increase to £45 per week.

* * *

City had just won the League Cup at Wembley when I signed. Dennis Tueart's overhead kick saw us to a 2-1 victory over Newcastle in February 1976. The club was on a roll and would finish runners-up to Liverpool in the league in 1976/77 and qualify for the UEFA Cup. There were stars all over the pitch and the profile was huge. That season only rivals United took the two points at Maine Road, with a 3-1 win in front of 49,000 on a September afternoon. We wouldn't lose at home for 13 months, when Wolves won

2-0. The football was free-flowing and the support backed us to the hilt.

People, however, were waiting for you to fail; I was at one of the biggest clubs in the country. I didn't have to be good, I had to be better than good because I was black. In the changing rooms or physio room you used to wait outside and knock the door before you went in. You couldn't just walk in. Today, it's all completely different. It was a huge learning curve. You had to show respect for the first-team players, and there were some greats in that changing room, players who ended up being my mates. The likes of Joe Corrigan, Dennis Tueart, one of the all-time greats Kazimierz Deyna, Tommy Booth, who I still see now, and Peter Barnes was later at Coventry with me. You had to learn the rules. Colin Bell was returning after his knee injury and was in every day for treatment and to use the gym. Those players accepted me, and it was great. They helped me, spoke to me, encouraged me.

We were coached by a big Scottish guy called Dave Ewing. He'd made over 300 appearances for the club between 1952 and 1962 and played in both the 1955 and 1956 FA Cup finals. Dave was hard as nails, and everybody who was at Maine Road knows about him. You could hear him for miles. He took me under his wing and with his tutelage I had to come in every day to do weights to build myself up. On the occasional day I didn't do extra, he'd know; he didn't miss a trick. We also had Len Heppel, who came in to do the fitness and movement work. He was the ballroom dance champion, along with his wife. Malcolm always told us to put your shoulders back and keep smiling.

When we had trialists in for practice matches we could kick them, but they couldn't kick us. It was to check out their temperament, how they dealt with pressure and intimidation, whether they could look after themselves. If I played against the reserves or the first team I couldn't kick them, but they could kick me as I was after their position; they were protecting their own spots in the respective starting line-ups. This was all part of the learning curve in my first year where I learned constantly. I did well and built up a good relationship with Roger Palmer, and we were one of the favourites to win the Youth Cup.

When I signed my contract late in November 1976 I didn't consider the effect of what I was achieving, a local lad from a West Indian community. My parents worked on the railways, and I'd started to get a few write-ups in the local paper. People started talking to my dad about it and would say, 'Your son is at Man City now, what's he doing there, playing sweeper?' As if I was on the ground staff sweeping the terraces, but that's how it was. The community looked after me, and growing up in Manchester you were either

THE EARLY YEARS: HOMETOWN HERO

United or City. I'd watched United but was turning into a true Blue, so when I played against the red side of the city you had to win at all costs. You'd have the milkman a City fan and the postman followed United. They knew who you were, and word went around; that was difficult, as even going to the local shop you were known. There was no hiding place, but this made you want to succeed and achieve so much, so it was a precious opportunity.

* * *

In 1977/78 I played for the reserves as we won the Central League title for the first time. I played 38 games and scored 18 times. It was while playing for the reserves that I began to train on the same pitch as the likes of Joe Royle, Gary Owen, Peter Barnes, Brian Kidd and Kenny Clements. There was a mutual trust on the pitch. Willie Donachie, Dave Watson, Colin Bell and Asa Hartford would see you on the training pitch. They knew they could trust you with the ball and they looked out for you on the pitch. If they didn't rate you, if you weren't any good, they wouldn't have paid you the respect they paid me. There were several older professionals in the reserves on their way back from injury, notably Colin Bell and Brian Kidd, Paul Power and Tony Henry. We won the title in the days when reserve-team football was tough and unforgiving; no one was in there to make up the numbers and we all had a goal. You learned your trade at this level, the tackles were flying in, they'd give you a rap on the ankles in training and your instinct was to react, but you just had to take it and get on with it, all part of the learning curve.

Roger Palmer top-scored with 20 and stepped up to the first team, scoring three times. He made his debut away to Middlesbrough, Christmas 1977, yet by October 1980 Oldham had signed him and, as we all know, he went on to become their all-time leading goalscorer over the next 14 seasons. Many City fans recall his hat-trick at Maine Road, August 1988, as Oldham thumped us 4-1. Ray Ranson, Henry and skipper Ged Keegan all played over 30 games in that Central League success, while the greats, Colin Bell and Mike Doyle, played 40 between them. Only Everton, Liverpool and Nottingham Forest finished above City in the First Division that season.

As 1977/78 concluded, Tony Book signed me on to a new contract. My season with the youth team and reserves had been a real success and I penned a one-year deal with the option of a second, which saw my money rise to £60 a week with a £20 bonus for appearing in the first team. Tony and Bill Taylor, the England coach, kept encouraging me, working to improve all aspects of my game. They wouldn't think twice about replacing you as there was always someone waiting in the wings. You needed the right temperament to deal with pressure and expectation. City was such a massive club in terms of its history, where it had been and where it was going. With United and the Merseyside clubs doing well, football was massive. You always had a chance in the game if City or United released you, as you had pedigree. The reputation of the clubs ensured you were sought after.

My old mate Peter Coyne scored the most goals in United's reserves, one of the best finishers I've ever seen – left foot, right foot. They told him to get his hair cut and he refused. When Tommy Docherty released him in the spring of 1977, he was still 18 and initially ended up at Ashton United before Crewe signed him in the summer and he was able to get back on the pitch, doing what he did best, scoring goals. He'd had the world at his feet, all the clubs had wanted his signature, the nation had seen his success at Wembley when he scored two hat-tricks for England Schoolboys. His brother, Ged, was on the books at City but there was no one else in my year who went on to turn professional.

While I continued to develop and progress in the reserves, the first team finished 15th in the First Division in 1978/79 and reached the quarter-finals of both cup competitions. Malcolm Allison returned in January 1979 as a coaching mentor to Tony Book, six years after leaving

Maine Road for Crystal Palace. He brought in a real emphasis on stretching and ensuring my hamstrings were in good condition. Along with many other players, Malcolm educated us to prepare in the correct way for matches.

Tony Book had signed Kazimierz Deyna just prior to Christmas. Deyna was one of the first wave of foreign players to play in the English league. He'd played at Wembley for Poland in 1973 when they knocked out England in the World Cup qualifier, and by 1978's tournament in Argentina he was captain. He'd retired from international football prior to joining us with 97 caps, and Zbigniew Boniek took his place as captain. 'Kazi', as he was known to us, was what you'd term a 'playmaker'. In his three seasons with us he appeared just 43 times, but seven goals in the last eight games of 1978/79 gave us momentum to stay in the top tier when it was looking slightly precarious in the spring. Brian Kidd used to comment on how Deyna was an excellent manipulator of the ball, so much guile, his technique was something else. He sadly passed away at the age of 41 after a car accident in his adopted home of San Diego, where he headed after leaving City in 1981, shortly before John Bond took charge. The Polish Football Association in later years voted him the best Polish player of all time. 'Kazi' left a positive impact on the players, the fans and the club in general.

My first-ever £20 bonus and senior debut came in the April at Maine Road as Gordon Lee's Everton visited. The team list would go up on a Friday and everyone would crowd around the board to see if they were in the 12; only one substitute then, of course. It was a moment I'll never forget for the right and wrong reasons. It gave me a taste for more; who wouldn't be inspired by playing in front of just under 40,000 at Maine Road? I'd played most of the Central League games that season too. After winning the title we finished fourth this time around, and in 35 appearances I scored 15 goals, with only goalkeeper Keith Macrae and defender Ray Ranson appearing more times. Tommy Caton was a regular, while Colin Bell played alongside us 23 times, with regular runs for Tony Henry, Ron and Paul Futcher, Nicky Reid, Steve Kinsey, Gary Buckley, Russell Coughlin and Roger Palmer, although his involvement with the first team became greater as the season progressed.

Malcolm took over from Tony Book in the summer of 1979, while Tony moved into the role of general manager. As City fans know, Tony is known universally as 'Skip' and he used to play in the five-a-sides, loving a slide-tackle. When Malcolm walked in the room you knew he was there, he had an aura about him. Whether he was sporting a big cigar or a hat, he had a passion in his eyes, a burning desire to win, to do well. Who wouldn't be drawn in and inspired by this? Malcolm always ensured you were well. He pushed all the young lads, me, Ray Ranson, Tommy Caton, Nicky Reid and Steve Mackenzie.

Steve arrived with a great reputation during that summer. Malcolm signed him for £250,000 from Crystal Palace, where he was an apprentice yet to break into the first team at Selhurst Park. He was the most expensive teenager when he joined, the irony being he made his City debut against Palace on the opening day of the season. Also making his first-team debut that day was 16-year-old Tommy Caton, alongside Tommy Booth at the heart of our defence.

Nicky Reid, another local lad, from Davyhulme, made his debut a month prior to me in much different circumstances. Malcolm named him in the team to face Borussia Mönchengladbach in our UEFA Cup draw at Maine Road. He also featured in the second leg defeat two weeks later, as the West Germans won 3-1 to move into the semi-finals. Mönchengladbach went on to win the trophy, defeating Red Star Belgrade 2-1 on aggregate in the final. Red Star had beaten West Brom at the quarter-final stage and Arsenal in the third round. Bear in mind Nicky was 18 and this was a quarter-final tie where he was up against the Dane, Allan Simonsen. Nicky got stuck in and never feared a challenge, and Malcolm threw him into one of our biggest games with Gary Owen injured. There were 39,000

THE EARLY YEARS: HOMETOWN HERO

in Maine Road under the lights but he just got on with it. We were team-mates in the Central League title win and there were parallels with our respective progress into the first-team squad.

Being so far advanced with all his various techniques, Malcolm had us playing three at the back. He'd bring us into the club early in the morning on matchdays and we'd train at 11am before the game at 3pm. He wanted to ensure we were wide awake and ready to go. The only downside was come half-time we were shattered. We had five in midfield, flowing football, and we were given the confidence to play different systems and to play the right way, entertaining and with flair in abundance. With all the training during the summer I was able to cope with the physicality of matchday, but I didn't feature in the matchday 12 as the season got underway. I kept up my form and fitness in the reserves, ready to take any opportunity that came my way but, before that could happen, Malcolm splashed the cash again, following on from the signing of Mackenzie.

Along with Steve Mackenzie, Malcolm had also signed striker Michael Robinson from Preston, who were then in the Second Division. The fee of £750,000 took the summer spending to the million-pound mark. It didn't stop there. We'd taken three points from the first four league games and Malcolm wanted Steve Daley in our side. He'd made over 200 appearances for Wolves, an attacking midfielder with an eye for goal. On 5 September the initial talks looked at a fee of £250,000, and bear in mind this was the era before agents. Steve was quite happy at Wolves, but we were a side packed with international players and it was a fresh and exciting challenge for him. Arsenal, Bobby Robson at Ipswich, Newcastle and Chelsea also showed interest, while Wolves were known to be after Villa's Andy Gray. John Barnwell, Wolves' manager, told Steve that a deal had been agreed with Peter Swales, so he hopped in his Ford Cortina and headed up the M6. The transfer fee just kept on rising through the day between Peter Swales and his counterpart in negotiations, and when Steve finally signed the deal it was an astronomical £1,437,500. The contract length? Ten years. On 8 September Wolves paid Villa £1.5m for Andy Gray, thus the transfer record had been broken for the second time in four days.

Mind you, during the summer, Malcolm had also sold Gary Owen to West Brom, followed six weeks later by Peter Barnes. Under Ron Atkinson, Albion had qualified for the UEFA Cup after a third-place finish. Mick Channon had also moved to Southampton, and he was our top scorer in 1978/79. Barnes and Owen were local lads and fan favourites who made just over a hundred appearances each. They had so much more to offer us, but Malcolm was in transition mode. On Steve's first day at training, we went out on to the pitches at 11am and he was passing it around, great technique, in a game of defence versus attack. A cross came in and he smashed it on the volley over Joe and into the side of the goal. We all thought, *What have we signed here!?* Malcolm ended training there and then: 'We'll finish on that note!' Steve was great, a real gem of a lad. I got to know him really well and we're good friends to this day.

After a 4-0 thumping at The Hawthorns, Malcolm gave me my full debut in a 3-0 win over Coventry at Maine Road. I kept my place for the draw with Sunderland in the League Cup but then Kazi returned from injury and scored in three of the next four games. I returned for the win over Forest, in the No.4 shirt, in place of Bobby Shinton, then scored my first senior goal in the 2-2 draw at Carrow Road. A moment I've never forgotten. The instant the ball hit the back of the net, simply brilliant. Our home crowd soared from just over 30,000 to 48,000 for the visit of Liverpool. This was the season Liverpool conceded just 16 goals in 42 league games. Ray Clemence kept 28 clean sheets, including one on this day as the Reds swept home four without reply.

The Big Match cameras were at Selhurst Park a week later as Terry Venables' 'Team of the 80s', Crystal Palace, beat us 2-0. You'll have seen this game on *The Big Match Revisited*; how we weren't awarded a penalty for a blatant foul on me I'll never know. My fortunes had a sharp upturn seven days later when I took home the man-of-the-match award from the 2-0 Manchester derby win. Tony Henry and Michael Robinson took the plaudits for us, with 50,000 inside Maine Road. My first derby, and Piccadilly Radio presented me with a bottle of Moët, a huge honour for me when you consider the players on both sides. Along with our lads, Corrigan, Caton, Booth, Kazi, Daley, Robinson and Paul Power, United's line-up saw Michael Robinson and me up against Kevin Moran and Martin Buchan, with the likes of Sammy McIlroy, Ray Wilkins, Steve Coppell and Mickey Thomas also in their starting line-up. There was no Joe Jordan that day. He'd missed the first part of the season through injury for a United side who were then top of the First Division.

I then had a steady run in the side as we moved into 1980. Our form was inconsistent – wins over Bolton, Derby and Everton compounded by defeats at Bristol City and Ipswich, before Brighton thumped us 4-1 in the last game of 1979, at the Goldstone Ground. In early December the FA Cup third-round draw had been made live on Radio 2, the usual Monday lunchtime, with us all crowded round the radio after training. It seemed like an eternity before our ball was drawn, away to Halifax Town at The Shay. They were then in the Fourth Division.

THE EARLY YEARS: HOMETOWN HERO

It was the last thing Malcolm needed. The pressure was building and he was in the spotlight even more than usual. Halifax had been re-elected to the Football League in two of the previous three seasons but had lost just once at home this season. The Shay pitch was an advantage to the Yorkshire side, and it had snowed all week in the run-up to the game. The pitch was ankle deep in water 48 hours prior, and their manager, George Kirby, had poured hundreds of gallons of extra water on to an already sodden surface. By the time we came to kick-off it was just about playable. Pitches like this in the 80s were ideal for an upset. The referee, Michael Lowe, gave it two inspections before lunch but you could just tell in the warm-up that it was going to be an uncomfortable afternoon. This was compounded by our back four, with Booth, Donachie and Futcher absent, so Nicky Reid partnered Tommy Caton in the centre, with Ray Ranson on the right and Paul Power on the left. The crowd of 13,000 was four times the normal attendance at The Shay and there wasn't room to move on a horrible day for watching football, let alone playing. They were no mugs either. Their players included Mick Kennedy, Lee Hendrie's dad, Paul, and captain Dave Evans, who'd joined them from Villa and was one of the Bradford players carrying people away from the fire on that awful day at Valley Parade.

With so much rain and the pitch a quagmire we couldn't play our usual quick passing game. Malcolm had insisted we play the tie, and the cameras sensed a giant-killing. Halifax were able to get close and press us, which ramped up the pressure on us as the clock ticked on. Bobby Shinton had a great opportunity for us from my cross before the moment we all feared happened on 75 minutes. Paul Hendrie's goal sent the ground into chaos. Malcolm was sat in the tiniest dugout imaginable as the celebrations went on around him. At the final whistle you could hear 'Allison out' and 'Swales out' from the City end, and Steve Daley copped an earful from supporters as he boarded the coach home. We were on *Match of the Day* so the whole nation witnessed the upset.

You never forget those days, and nine years later I'd face even worse in a Coventry shirt. Any City fan who was there will never forget that day and neither will the many thousands listening on the radio or following on *Grandstand*. Martin Tyler summed up the match, writing in *The Times*: 'It had every element of cup-tie football: the Fourth Division against the First; the poor of the league against the biggest spenders; a quagmire of a pitch in one of the game's least fashionable settings.' For the City fans on the terrace on a rainy, sodden day in West Yorkshire, they could only dream of their club's current fortunes: from

THE EARLY YEARS: HOMETOWN HERO

Shinton to Sergio, Weaver to Ederson, life has always been eventful on the blue side of Manchester.

Fortunately, we didn't live in the 24/7 social media world we do now. The Sunday papers reported the game then the Monday saw the draw for the fourth round. Peter Swales described the result as the worst day of his football life. He backed Malcolm and Tony to the hilt in person and with money. Halifax drew Bolton at Burnden Park and lost 2-0. Bolton went out after a replay to Arsenal in the fifth round.

* * *

It's fair to say the defeat rocked us as we didn't win another game until 12 April. March had seen Malcolm react to our struggles, as Dennis Tueart returned from a spell with New York Cosmos, while Kevin Reeves signed from Norwich for £1.25m. At the time, Malcolm compared him to Kevin Keegan and praised Peter Swales for opening the chequebook again. After Trevor Francis, Steve Daley and Andy Gray, Kevin was the fourth-most expensive player of all time. No pressure then. Joe Corrigan really rated Kevin, as we all did, and we saw the difference his play made to the side. Paul Sugrue was brought in from Nuneaton Borough, then in the Alliance Premier, the equivalent today of the National League. He was signed for £30,000 and tipped as the new sensation. On the final day of the season, he made his debut alongside Kevin in our 2-1 win over Ipswich. Along with Paul there were several young players trying to make their mark at City. Gary Buckley was the brother of Mick, who played up at Sunderland. Gary joined us after rave reviews and was tipped for the very top. We also had Ronnie Evans, and Nicky Reid who, like me, had made his debut in 1978/79 and pushed on this year.

I played most of the games after Halifax, including the Manchester derby defeat at Old Trafford – 56,000 in attendance that day. Three wins out of the last four games steadied us, as we finished 17th, six points off the relegation zone. I didn't add to my two goals at Norwich but appeared 27 times in total. Our struggles were highlighted by Michael Robinson top-scoring with just nine goals, followed by Paul Power with seven. Little did we realise that the following season was going to take us within a whisker of glory.

2

On My Way to Wembley

IT'S FAIR to say 1980/81 didn't start well. Michael Robinson had left for Brighton during the summer. Dennis Tueart's return had effectively taken his place. Bear in mind that Michael was 21 when Malcolm signed him, and he scored nine in 35 appearances for City in mostly a season of struggle. We only took four points from the opening 12 league games and only won in the League Cup with success over Stoke and away at Luton. Paul Sugrue wore No.9 for the opening three league games, defeats against Southampton and Sunderland and a draw with Villa.

My first appearance of the season came at Ayresome Park, wearing No.7 in a 2-2 draw with Middlesbrough. The League Cup replay with Stoke saw me open my account with two goals in a 3-0 victory, and I kept my place until the start of October, missing the 3-0 defeat at Maine Road to Liverpool. Malcolm was sacked after the next game, a

1-0 defeat at Leeds. He'd only been back for 15 months but we were languishing one off the bottom, with only Terry Venables' Palace below us. When he left, Malcolm came back to Platt Lane, our training ground, and shook everybody by the hand. He had faith and belief in you, and you knew you could make it work after being managed by the great man.

Tony Book was asked to stay on as caretaker manager while a replacement was found. This was 8 October, then John Bond took over nine days later. From when he took the manager's role in the spring of 1974, Tony won the League Cup and we finished runners-up in the league, missing the title by one point. Peter Swales and the board were desperate for success and to be the number one club in Manchester. It was a regret for Peter that the change was made; hindsight's great, of course. Who knows what would have happened if Malcolm hadn't been brought back and Tony had been left to carry on his good work?

John Bond was flamboyant and a good fit for City. He'd done well at Norwich and had a big focus on attitude. He held himself well but, if he needed to let off steam, he was well capable and made sure you knew the point he was making. Confidence was low when he arrived and we lost his first game. I was up front with Kevin Reeves. However, after a couple of weeks on the training ground with John we won four games on the bounce. He took us back to basics and brought in three key signings for us: Bobby McDonald and Tommy Hutchison from Coventry and Gerry Gow from Bristol City. By January, John had won two manager of the month awards and we'd lost just twice. The structure of the team changed as many of the new signings were cup-tied, so it was almost Malcolm's team in the League Cup and John's in the league. Fresh ideas came from McDonald and Hutchison, and Gerry Gow was a real competitor, a fierce ball-winner in the midfield. Not many relished a battle with him, and all three signings were popular, well-received additions both by fans and players.

Tommy Hutchison remembers well his departure from Highfield Road:

> I'd got a bit of flak when I left for Maine Road. Gordon Milne had left me out of the Coventry side for a game at Leicester. I'd only just returned from a summer with Seattle Sounders in the North American Soccer League (NASL). I told Gordon I wouldn't play in the reserves; I was 33 at the time and would rather go elsewhere and play for someone week in, week out. I'd agreed with Seattle manager Alan Hinton that I would return there but then the next week Coventry

were at home to Norwich, who'd just lost John Bond to Manchester City, and I was in the players' lounge with Bobby McDonald talking to Kevin Bond, Norwich's right-back, who I'd met over the summer in Seattle as he was a mate of John Ryan, Norwich's left-back, who'd been a team-mate of mine over the summer. I said to Kevin his dad would need a left-winger, and Bobby Mac said he'll need a left-back too. Bobby had just come off the back of 178 consecutive appearances at Coventry but had also just lost his place after a fall-out.

I thought no more of it until the Monday morning when I got called to Gordon's office. I couldn't work out how they were going to let me go to City, who were second bottom of the league, but I agreed to go and speak to them, with no intention of signing because I'd agreed to go back to Seattle but hadn't signed anything concrete. I went and spoke to John Bond, who asked me how much I wanted. I bought some time as I needed to speak to my family; the money John offered was something else and he asked me to call my wife there and then. I thought I was in too deep straight away so I had to tell John that

I'd promised Seattle I wouldn't sign for anyone else unless I'd spoken to them first. He wouldn't let me leave until I signed the contract, and said he'd tear it up if I came back to him after talking to Seattle and said 'no'.

I called Alan Hinton at Seattle and told him I was going to join City; the chance to play for a big club like them at 33 years of age was something I just couldn't turn down. The way it was written in the press made it look like I had called Coventry a small club, but the press got it wrong, and I have apologised to the supporters since. I could see why Coventry were losing players because we'd hit as high as we could. The club didn't have the money to move to the next stage. I thought I'd finish my career at Coventry, but if they'd kept me past the end of the season they wouldn't have received any money for me as I turned 34 then. As it transpired, Coventry only got £47,500 for me in the deal with Bobby. That summer of 1980 in Seattle, I earned more in that couple of months than in the rest of my career, it was crazy money.

Our first league win arrived on 22 October, under the lights for the visit of Tottenham. How our respective paths would cross in months to come. Gary Buckley made his debut in a 3-1 win, with goals from Daley, Mackenzie and Reeves. Close to 30,000 were there as Bond's arrival gave the club a real lift. Three days later Bobby and Tommy made their debuts, replacing Buckley and Tommy Booth in a Dennis Tueart-inspired win at Brighton. I was left out for these two games and returned for the Notts County cup clash, when I got back on the scoresheet along with Dennis, who scored four times that night to take us into round four.

Dennis took me under his wing at City. A very articulate man, he had a fiery temperament but taught me what to do and when. It was a real-life lesson for me at a young age, 21 then. He wasn't the type of guy to cross and gave me a lot of his time, for which I was always grateful. It was a mantra I carried on into my career, helping the younger players. At the end of training he'd always take three penalties and Joe Corrigan used to hate it. If you ever chipped Joe he'd race over and punch you. He'd take such pride in getting his angles right and you always wanted to end the session with the ball hitting the net, the ripple as you smashed it home. I did it in every warm-up prior to a game – start the way you mean to carry on. Repetition was key, practise, practise, practise, ensure you trained at the same intensity you played on a Saturday.

I've heard similar stories about Big Joe from players at Coventry. Peter Bodak famously chipped him in the FA Cup at Maine Road then joined City at the end of that season. He was all chirpy in the tunnel afterwards and Paul Dyson recalled having to push Peter into the dressing room to avoid Joe from their days at Stoke: 'Joe would say he was there to save shots, so of course everyone used to chip him. He'd go barmy.' When Peter joined Joe at Maine Road he'd chip him at every opportunity in training: 'He'd chase me round the training ground but thankfully never caught me!'

As we moved into November, further points were accumulated with a win over Norwich. It would be the last time Steve Daley stepped out in City colours after just 14 months at the club. He tried so hard to make it work. He was trying everything to justify the fee, which wasn't his fault in any way, but the media were on to him constantly and the fans expected so much each time he stepped on to the pitch, but it never deterred him. In all he appeared 54 times for us and scored four goals. Seattle Sounders in the NASL subsequently signed Steve, who was then aged 27. If he had his time again in Manchester, I know he'd approach it differently; it was almost like right club, wrong time. Gerry Gow took over Steve's No.8 shirt and their styles contrasted greatly.

After a defeat up at Sunderland we bounced back with three straight league wins and took the momentum into December. I'd added a couple of goals against Southampton and Coventry before we faced West Brom in the quarter-final of the League Cup, where we saw a crowd of over 35,000. Cyrille Regis, Remi Moses and Brendon Batson were in their side that night, one of the best Albion teams. Cyrille and I knew of each other as there weren't many black players in the First Division. Clyde Best had played in the 70s for West Ham, Garth Crooks was starting out at Stoke and Viv Anderson at Forest. In the Second Division, Bob Hazell was at QPR and George Berry at Wolves. Vince Hilaire had shone in recent years at Palace, so we were making an impact but getting a lot of abuse at grounds like Stamford Bridge and Upton Park. Brian Stein and Ricky Hill would get promoted with Luton, while Pedro Richards and Tristan Benjamin were at Notts County and would soon be joined by John Chiedozie. It was harder for players like me who were on their own, whereas if there were two or three of you there was support and you could talk. We were laying the foundations for more and more black players to appear on the scene, opening doors with our achievements.

We beat Albion 2-1 to reach the semi-finals, with goals from myself and Tony Henry. John Bond handed a debut that night to Phil Boyer, one of his trusted strikers from his

Carrow Road days. Phil had been at Southampton for the last three seasons, and John, already reunited with Kevin Reeves, added him to the squad. He was an ever-present until a serious knee injury during an FA Cup tie against, ironically, Norwich, in mid-January, which saw his season ended. Whenever we played Albion, I always had a good game against Derek Statham, who was a terrific player and very unlucky over the years not to pick up more than three England caps. During his retirement he was voted one of Albion's 16 greatest-ever players. No mean feat given the class of the side under Big Ron's management.

After the Albion win, I was sidelined through injury and missed a further run of four straight wins: Leeds, Everton, Wolves and then Palace in the FA Cup third round. These were the days when you played both on Boxing Day and 27 December. Luckily the fixtures computer used common sense with us away at Everton then home the next day to Wolves. It wasn't always the case, as years later at Coventry we travelled to QPR then back home for Tottenham the next day. You didn't have this routine every year, just when dates dictated. Phil Boyer was in the No.7 shirt during this time, but I was back in the side for the League Cup semi-final against Liverpool. Gerry Gow was cup-tied, and we had a strong side out that night, with 48,000 in Maine Road for the first leg.

The draw hadn't done us any favours. At the time Liverpool were unbeatable and we were unlucky to not draw Coventry or Second Division West Ham. Bobby McDonald and Tommy were also cup-tied. Gary Buckley was on the bench. We went for them from the first whistle. Kevin Reeves scored a perfectly good goal in the opening minutes; he rose above Alan Kennedy, who collided with Ray Clemence. The ball went into the net. Reeves didn't get near to Clemence but referee Alf Grey disallowed it and we were stunned. The stadium went berserk. It was the perfect start, a bit like when they score nowadays and VAR then spoils everything. The irony was that Liverpool's goal came from a disputed free kick from which Ray Kennedy scored nine minutes from time. We'd seen the home leg as our chance to build an advantage to take to Anfield; it was a real injustice. We'd played well too. Big Joe was in fine form, Tommy Caton and Nicky Reid solid against Fairclough and Dalglish. Tony Henry battled against Souness and McDermott, while I felt I had a good game and caused them problems.

I was back on the bench for the 3-2 win over Middlesbrough, John Bond's changes bearing fruit as both Tommy and Bobby were on the scoresheet. John was helping me improve as a player, along with his assistant, John Benson. They were always encouraging me, telling me to look for the flick-ons, gamble, take a chance, press the centre-halves. Three into two often didn't go with Kevin and Dennis, and Kevin was always going to feature, given his transfer fee. But I learned so much from these lads, and my game was steadily improving. Next up in the FA Cup fourth round were Norwich and the crowds were starting to build; you could feel the momentum. Just shy of 39,000 watched but we lost Phil Boyer early on with his season-ending knee injury. The irony was that John Bond's son, Kevin, collided with him, then eight months later he'd be his team-mate. Steve Mackenzie fired in a cracker from 25 yards and then we had a late flurry of goals, including one from me, to win 6-0.

Monday morning at training we were all sat around the radio, ready for the draw at lunchtime. The fifth round would take us away to Peterborough just four days after the League Cup second leg at Anfield as we strived for Wembley. Peterborough at the time were in the Fourth Division, so it brought immediate thoughts of Halifax. We'd be on a hiding to nothing, the expectation being that we'd sail through to the quarter-finals. They had a young lad in midfield, Micky Gynn, small, quick, who was starting to make a name for himself. Before the trip to London Road, however, we had a trip in the league to Aston Villa. They were challenging Bobby Robson's Ipswich for the title and took a further two points with Gary Shaw's early goal. We then held European champions Nottingham Forest to a draw at Maine Road before going off to Liverpool, trailing 1-0 after the first leg.

It was my 50th appearance for the club and I was back in the starting XI. So too was Gary Buckley, with Tony Henry on the bench. We were on the back foot early on after Kenny Dalglish extended the aggregate lead, but a Kevin Reeves goal brought us back into the tie just after half-time. We gave it everything and threw on Tony for Ray Ranson with 15 minutes to go, but just couldn't get the elusive goal. Bar Alan Kennedy, Liverpool were at full strength, as they weren't in the title race and certainly didn't want to end the season without silverware. I'd scored five goals during the cup run in the previous four ties but just couldn't add to the tally against Liverpool. We still felt wronged after the disallowed goal in the first leg, and even Graeme Souness had spoken to the press to state that 'City's no goal looked good'. We certainly weren't overawed in the two ties and left Merseyside determined to get the expected result at Peterborough in four days' time.

For a Fourth Division club, I know it was the fifth round of the cup, but just under 28,000 watched the tie, a phenomenal number, only a couple of thousand off the all-time club record. The City fans were packed in behind the goal where Tommy Booth scored the winner after a scramble following a corner. It would prove to be Tommy's last goal for the club but what a vital one it was. You always know in this kind of tie that your opponents will come out all guns blazing, real pressure from the kick-off, and you just need to keep your shape and discipline and start to dominate possession. Invariably they'll tire as the game moves on and that's when mistakes creep in and you take advantage, as we did here. The corner wasn't cleared, it bounced around and then Tommy smashed it into the roof of the net. I'd had a decent chance prior to this, which was denied, but we dealt with the occasion well and to get into another quarter-final, especially the FA Cup, was a real bonus. We had belief it could be our year.

It was Manchester derby day next up for us, at home, 50,000 watching. I know I mention the crowds a lot but the atmosphere at Maine Road was something else, and when you've got this amount of support roaring you on it's like a goal start. Steve Mackenzie was beginning to flourish in midfield, giving the team stability, but he also possessed the ability to contribute important goals. The No.9 shirt was his and his form belied his years. Steve scored the winner against United. We had a patient build-up, I laid it out to Paul Power, whose pass was right into the path of Mackenzie, who smashed it past a motionless Gary Bailey.

A goal to win any game and it kept our fine form going with an exciting end to the season in store.

Maine Road was a big ground, the pitch one of the largest in the league, and we used the width to our advantage. Sitting at the scoreboard end was Helen Turner, the 'bell' lady. Before each game she used to give Joe a sprig of heather for luck. When the team was down or when she thought we needed lifting, she'd ring the bell. It was such a significant moment each time, and I've never witnessed anything like it since. At the last-ever game at Maine Road, against Southampton, she famously rang it for the last time and the ground stood to applaud her.

After defeat at Highbury, we were all set for the FA Cup quarter-final with Everton at Goodison. I wasn't in the squad that day. Dennis was up front with Kevin Reeves. The ground was packed, over 50,000 there. It was a real blood-and-thunder cup tie, end to end, with a bit of controversy at the close when Kevin Ratcliffe butted Tommy Hutchison and saw red. Just a minute earlier Paul Power had levelled at 2-2 to take it back to Maine Road. John Bond kept the same 12 for the replay four days later. There was a similar huge crowd again, but this time our experience counted. Goalless just after the hour, two goals from Bobby Mac and again Paul Power saw us through. We'd been looked at as one of the weak sides in the draw, but we had players who'd played at the top level for many years, and we were wise. There had been numerous pitch inspections on the day of the replay, with so much rain in Manchester. The pitch was a mess but we'd almost become used to it and ensured we kept the ball wide where there was grass – almost played to the pitch's strengths.

You can imagine the atmosphere around the club as the semi-final draw paired us with Ipswich at Villa Park. Before that we had half a dozen league fixtures, where I featured sporadically, back in the starting XI for the 3-3 with Leicester at Maine Road. We all knew, however, just how big the Ipswich tie would be, as they were toe to toe with Villa for the title and had moved into the semi-finals of the UEFA Cup, where they'd already beaten Cologne away from home to lead the tie. Three days later we met at Villa Park, one of the all-time favourite neutral venues, and I was back in the side. John Bond went for my pace and speed in place of Dennis. I'd battled hard to stay in the team after playing in the League Cup ties but sometimes my play wasn't good enough. Phil had come in from Souuthampton but his injury gave me a chance to feature, and I knew I had to play well against Ipswich, with Terry Butcher, Kevin Beattie and Russell Osman in direct opposition.

Little did we know it would be Beattie's last game for Ipswich. He had three or four headers from set pieces, and

Tommy cleared one off the line early on. He was so good in the air, Beattie. They were dominant approaching the half-hour and then the likes of Gerry Gow wrestled back the initiative, going close as half-time loomed. They'd missed several chances, but Tommy and Nicky Reid were in fine form against Brazil and Mariner, and we went in level.

During the season, Ipswich played 66 games, and they really were a team of superstars. Paul Cooper kept over 25 clean sheets, Osman, Thijssen, Wark and Mariner were named in the Professional Footballers' Association (PFA) First Division Team of the Year, while Wark won the PFA Players' Player award. They were focused, while our side was full of enthusiasm and had nothing to lose – safe in the league, this was our goal. Could we handle how good Ipswich were on the day? For some of us it was our first big game. The UEFA Cup run in 1978/79 had seen opportunities for Big Joe, Paul Power and Nicky, and we were used to big crowds, but not big occasions where the game was on TV. Everyone was glued to the FA Cup. In the 1980s those games were always fantastic, full of drama and excitement, a great spectacle, where scoring the winner made you a household name. As a kid you dream of days like these. Not many players play in a semi-final so you must savour the moment but make sure you don't let the opportunity slip by.

Into the second half and Ipswich had their chances, Kevin Beattie a threat every time he went into our penalty area. He must have felt it wasn't going to be his day when he crashed into me late in the half and had to be replaced. It later transpired he'd broken his arm and missed the two-legged UEFA Cup Final when Ipswich beat AZ Alkmaar. He had an amazing spring when he jumped to head the ball and we so nearly suffered at his hands. Tommy Caton was brilliant that day, and in no small part his duel with Beattie was a key factor as the score remained 0-0. We went into extra time.

We attacked the Holte End for the first period, and ten minutes in Terry Butcher collided with me after I'd won a ball that wasn't mine to win. It was just to the right of centre and prime position for a move Steve Mackenzie and Paul Power had worked on in training. By changing the angle slightly, Steve gave Paul the chance to whip the ball up and over the wall, and it dipped over Paul Cooper into the bottom corner. Fabulous strike. There were City fans everywhere; it took a while to clear the pitch. The goal lifted us, energy-wise, and shattered Ipswich. Their socks were round their ankles. We had 20 minutes to see out and then a visit to Wembley was ours. When the final whistle went, I'll never forget the scenes, even now after all these years. I was 21 and hoped I was going to walk out at

Wembley, but we had four league games to play and only 12 shirts to fill.

The trip to Wolves couldn't have gone better for me with two goals in our 3-1 win. We trailed to a John Richards goal within a minute, but Dennis crashed in a volley and then I smashed in a couple of close-range efforts to take the points late on. It was a similar result on Easter Monday as Everton came to Maine Road. Another goal for me and the last appearance for Paul Sugrue. It hadn't really worked out for him and, after he'd scored goals galore for Nuneaton, he just couldn't reproduce it at City, so in the summer he moved to Cardiff City.

A week later and it was Gary Buckley's last game for us as Ipswich avenged the cup defeat with a 1-0 win at Portman Road. Gary moved to Preston, then in the Third Division. Another youth player, Andy May, made his debut, replacing Gary.

The goals couldn't have come at a better time for me as I netted again in a draw with Palace. Wembley was a week away and I'd scored in three of the four matches since the semi-final. I was desperate to play in the final. It didn't bother me whether it was in midfield or up front, as long as I was out on that pitch. John Bond had helped me to improve as the season progressed; he was a winner and drove us all on.

The FA had announced before the final that if it should go to a replay, the cup would then be decided on penalties, not go to a second replay. John Bond was furious; he just couldn't understand why they'd made such a decision. With it being the 100th final the FA also announced, if required, a replay would be on the Thursday, the day after England played Brazil in a friendly. In previous years the only replay had been at Old Trafford when Chelsea beat Leeds.

Saturday, 9 May 1981. John Bond led us out on to the Wembley turf. I was wearing No.7, up front with Kevin Reeves. Paul Power and Tommy on the wings, Steve Mackenzie and Gerry in the middle. Tommy Caton and Nicky Reid, 18 and 20 respectively, the youngest-ever centre-back pairing in an FA Cup Final, they were that good. Ray Ranson and Bobby McDonald at full-back, with Tony Henry on the bench that day. Tottenham had finished tenth in the league, strong at home, and beaten QPR, Hull, Coventry, Exeter and Wolves en route to the final. We'd had the more difficult path to the twin towers, although the likes of Glenn Hoddle, Ossie Ardiles, Ricky Villa, Garth Crooks and Steve Archibald were a match for anyone.

Our captain Paul Power introduced us to the Queen Mother, and referee Keith Hackett called him and Steve Perryman to the centre circle. I was the first black player to represent City in an FA Cup Final and proud of it. We had two shirts each, one short-sleeved, one long-sleeved, and I wore long-sleeved, like I did in 1987. The pitch was heavy and there had been plenty of rain. Tottenham struggled for the first hour. I thought we were in control and deserved the lead when Tommy's flying header set Wembley alight. It was brilliant, a great ball in from Ray Ranson and brave as well from Tommy to beat Graham Roberts to the cross.

Shortly after, Steve Mackenzie hit the post – how he could influence a game. He could strike a ball and would try anything on the pitch. He was similar in life. If he could turn his hand to something he would. Many of the lads thought he gave us something different that season. If his shot had gone in, we'd have been two up with 30 minutes to play. However, Tottenham picked up straight away, the energetic Garry Brooke replacing Ricky Villa and Glenn Hoddle starting to assume control.

With ten minutes to go Gerry clipped Ossie for a free kick in Hoddle territory. Big Joe lined up his wall, but Perryman changed the angle, so Tommy peeled off the wall behind us. Before we knew it, his shoulder changed the ball's direction. Joe had it covered initially but it flew into the opposite corner. Tommy will say he's not the goalscorer who netted at both ends at Wembley; he scored at the same end. He looked shattered, on his haunches, as Tottenham celebrated a lucky reprieve.

Extra time was played almost at walking pace towards the end, as they were out on their feet and we just couldn't create an opportunity to win it. Tommy Hutchison had been replaced by Tony Henry at half-time in extra time. We'd seen how Brooke had lifted them when he replaced Villa, so John was hoping for similar with Tony. Graham Roberts was also struggling after he lost two teeth in a collision with Chris Hughton, which made a right mess, but he got up and carried on and was one of their better players on the day. How those players made it up to the Royal Box to meet the Queen Mother I'll never know, and then we had to walk past the cup, which was certainly an anticlimax. Tottenham took a fair bit of criticism for their performance, but we gave it a real go and made it difficult for them.

ITV's commentator on the day was Brian Moore, assisted by Jack Charlton. Now remember there were only two black players on the pitch, but Jack knew Garth Crooks's name but not mine. Commentators prepare for their matches in advance, do their research and make sure they know all the players. The FA Cup Final was the showpiece occasion of the season, everybody watched it and can remember the results and who scored the goals of all the finals in the 80s. The programme started at 9am, there was coverage from the team hotels and then on the coaches for the drive to the stadium. The only two foreign players among the sides were Ardiles and Villa, and this really amplified the build-up.

To then have a commentator call me 'the little coloured boy' and to not know my name was a lack of respect for me and my family. We couldn't say or do anything, it was almost as if it was alright to say this. In 2016, BT Sport was showing repeats of the highlights from the FA Cup finals. I slammed the decision to wipe the 'little coloured boy' remark from the coverage. There was a complaint to Ofcom and the term was ruled derogatory so should be removed from future screenings. The removal of the remark was rewriting history, in my opinion, and I wanted football fans to hear the language I was subjected to as a player. Watching the clip will show children nowadays that racist language was commonplace, even from famous people on the television. It shows what we had to tolerate back then, and you can't edit history. It was an old-fashioned comment and commonplace in 1981.

The replay was five days later. In their wisdom the FA put tickets on sale in London so Tottenham fans snapped them up; it was three to one, no fair split like normal. Tottenham fans were everywhere, and this caused problems in the stadium. City fans were outnumbered and there was trouble on the terraces. Segregation was non-existent on a cold, damp night. The pitch had taken a battering the previous night with England's game, but this time round the match ignited within minutes. Dennis was a late switch on the bench instead of Tony Henry, while Tottenham were unchanged. Ricky Villa kept his place just days after leaving the pitch in tears when he was substituted. Eight minutes in and he pounced on a rebound to fire them into the lead. We'd started the game superbly, Steve Mackenzie having a shot cleared off the line by Chris Hughton, showing the value of the man on the post at corners. Kevin Reeves then saw Villa block his chance from the resultant corner. Villa's goal came after some magic by Ossie on the left edge of our box, a deflection taking it into the path of Steve Archibald, whose snap shot was bravely blocked by Joe, only for a ricochet to give Villa an open goal. Tommy Caton and I had no chance trying to stop it. Why I was last man I've no idea.

Three minutes later and a moment of genius. Ray Ranson's long free kick was cleared by Paul Miller across his own box to Ossie, who headed it to Tommy, poised on the right edge of the Spurs penalty area. I can only describe it as a volleyball style 'set' as Tommy, on one knee, headed it square to Steve. It was a perfect lay-off and what outstanding technique to volley that ball into the top corner. Aleksic hardly moved. We all knew Steve had the technique but to utilise it on the big stage was something else.

The pace of the game never relented. Hoddle hit the post with a free kick before controversy arose, indirectly involving me. Ray launched a long ball in between Roberts and Miller. I was favourite to reach it just outside the penalty area, when Aleksic came flying out like Superman to clear. Quite a few of our lads carried on playing as they thought he'd headed it clear, but he'd punched it. Nowadays it would be a straight red, but it was different in 1981. Keith Hackett used discretion, according to commentator John Motson, and didn't even book him. The subsequent free kick went over the bar and the chance had gone. Big Joe then saved a piledriver from Villa and another shot with his feet from Tony Galvin. It was end to end, great to play in, absorbing to watch. And all this before half-time.

At the break John said he wanted us to press from the restart like we'd done in the first half and take the game to them. A long kick from Joe was flicked on unchallenged by Kevin Reeves, and I was already anticipating where it was heading. Just like John Bond and John Benson wanted from me upon their arrival. I was into my stride and took it slightly away from goal as Paul Miller drew level with me. His right arm went across then he nudged me into Chris Hughton, who was round on the cover. I couldn't stay on my feet as Hughton completed the job, and Keith Hackett was in no doubt. Like I said, I was going away from the goal, they could have stood up, no need to make any contact, as I couldn't get a shot away as they were both right next to me. Miller wasn't happy as Reeves put the penalty right into the corner.

Our name was on the cup, but a Hoddle-inspired Tottenham came right back at us. Tommy Caton had earlier been booked, the first person to be booked in both a final and the replay. Gerry Gow joined him, the fifth of the game, after he took out Ossie. Just as Keith was talking to him, Gerry's eye was distracted by the appearance of a fan right next to him. He was having a go at Gerry, having jumped the barriers. Keith to his credit stood in between them and called the police on to unceremoniously take the lad away. You didn't expect a pitch invader at Wembley in the FA Cup Final.

The clock was ticking, and we survived claims for a penalty after a corner landed on Tommy's arm. With VAR we'd have stood no chance, but Keith waved play on and we were lucky. A bit of Hoddle magic drew them level. He played a pass like a golf shot, with backspin, which held up in the turf enough for Garth Crooks to level with 70 minutes on the clock. The penalty appeal a distant memory, Tony Galvin then picked up the ball just outside their box and ran and ran and ran. He was out wide on the left and Ray forced him to check inside, where he found Villa.

He ran towards our defence, past Tommy, past Ray, past Tommy again and then somehow squeezed his shot under Joe. Just 25 minutes earlier our name had been on the cup.

Now Dennis Tueart was thrown on for Bobby McDonald, and he fired straight at Aleksic before smashing a volley past the right-hand post. We knew it was close, you only had to see Dennis's reaction. Moments later the final whistle was blown. It was a day when you could share the fans' emotions. We'd been so close in the first game and had led in the replay. You don't often see a goal like Steve Mackenzie's end up on the losing side. If it wasn't for Villa's solo goal taking the plaudits, we'd have heard so much more about that volley, it was that good.

The following Tuesday, five days later, we played our final league game of the season. Liverpool faced Real Madrid in the European Cup Final in eight days' time and, along with their League Cup win and ties in Europe, would play 61 games that season. With our success in both cups, we were now due to play our 57th game, at Anfield. Paul Power was involved in all 57, Kevin Reeves 54, Steve Mackenzie 53, Nicky Reid and Joe Corrigan 51. I was again in the starting XI and featured in 37 of the 57 games. In all I'd scored 13, with only Kevin Reeves on 17 above me. We ran out to a half-full Anfield and lost to Ray Kennedy's first-half goal. The game would be the last in a City shirt for Steve Mackenzie and for me, although neither of us had any inkling as we boarded the team bus for Manchester at the season's end.

Christmas 1979 had seen me sign a new contract that would take me through to July 1983. My basic money had risen to £125 a week, with the first-team appearance bonus of £75. There was also the added incentive of a wage rise if I was selected for the England Under-21 squad. This was yet to happen, but I really felt I'd improved under John Bond's management, and the season had gone so well for me and the club. I looked forward to 1981/82 and what it would bring. As it turned out, it would bring my departure from Maine Road.

3

Off to the Valleys

JUST A few weeks after the season ended, Martin O'Neill signed from Norwich City. He was 30 the following March but had a fine pedigree, with a league title and two European Cup winners' medals while at Nottingham Forest and he was a regular in the Northern Ireland side. He also wore the No.7 shirt.

Throughout the summer there were rumours that John Bond wanted to sign Trevor Francis. He'd recovered from a torn Achilles tendon, which had sidelined him for six months and caused him to miss the 1980 European Cup Final with Forest. The warning signs were visible just prior to the season's beginning when Steve Mackenzie was sold to West Brom, the reason being to finance a move for Francis. Trevor had already moved from Birmingham to Forest for £1m, the first million-pound player. Now he was set to move again, for £1.2m. John Bond stuck his neck on the line to sign him, to maintain and push on from the progress made last season. This was now early September and the season had already begun. It had started without Trevor, and it had also started without me.

Phil Boyer was back after his knee injury and wore No.9, alongside Kevin. Martin O'Neill wore No.7, with Dennis in place of the injured Gerry Gow. The team was unchanged for the draw at Notts County before a day at Stoke that thousands of City fans will never forget. John Bond had sealed the deal for Trevor, who drove up to Stoke to meet us at the Victoria Ground. The first time he met the lads was in the dressing room. He'd signed on the Thursday then gone back to Nottingham, where he lived. On the Friday he actually trained at Forest and finished with shooting practice, Peter Shilton in goal for him. Phil Boyer made way for Trevor, who scored twice that day. Over 10,000 City fans were there, an incredible atmosphere, as we won 3-1. But still I wasn't in the matchday squad. It was heart-breaking for me, no one had said anything and our new signing was wearing the No.7 shirt I'd worn at Wembley.

After a draw with Southampton, the first-team squad went to Norway for a lucrative friendly with Rosenborg. John Bond was playing two up front and I was up against Trevor and Kevin, both brought in for big transfer fees, so he had to play them. It was one of those things where three into two doesn't go, but nobody told me. John was there also on a scouting mission to watch the international Åge Hareide, but Peter Swales had other plans for me.

Peter asked me if I'd help his fellow chairman at Cardiff City, Bob Grogan, a friend of his. Cardiff were then in the Second Division and my brother Gary had left City two weeks earlier to sign for them. Peter told me I could come back to City, so that was why I went, on the premise that I could go back, like a loan move. I did wonder why all this was going on while John Bond was away. When John found out he was furious and sent me a telegram to tell me that he didn't want me to leave. Of course, it wasn't a loan move, it was a two-year deal and there was a clause in the move to give City first option to buy me back. It made it easy to settle in with Gary there. I only really went down there because he'd joined recently and was enjoying it. I know City fans were surprised when I left – it was a surprise to myself!

Trevor Francis played 29 games in total and scored 14 times. At Christmas, City were in the top four but he suffered a few injuries in the New Year and their form fell away. Martin O'Neill was back at Norwich after just six months at Maine Road and Trevor, after a successful 1982 World Cup, was sold to Sampdoria as City's finances struggled. For me, however, on 19 September 1981 I was on the train down to Cardiff. Only four months earlier I had been playing in the FA Cup Final.

Moving away from home was a big thing for me. I went thinking that I'd end up going back to Man City because that's what they'd said. I thought I wasn't playing at City at the time so I'd take one step back to then take two steps forward. The journey down was a real eye-opener, looking out the train window I couldn't see a football pitch anywhere. Two weeks previously my brother had moved to Cardiff from City, the arrival of Kevin Bond a big factor in his lack of game time. Gary recalls:

> When John Bond came in there was a big turnaround of players. I was knocking at the first-team door at this time when he brought his son, Kevin, to the club, who played in my position. I'd played regularly in the Central League and John called me into his office at the end of the 1980/81 season to tell me they were not going to offer me a new contract. He wanted to do things differently and my whole world fell apart. Dave was there to support me, as was Tony Book. Skip spoke to me and said there were a couple of clubs interested and one of them was Cardiff, where he had been doing some work. I went down there on trial,

played well and the manager, Richie Morgan, told me he wanted to sign me on a three-year contract. When I signed the contract, however, there was no mention at all of Dave joining me.

Paul Sugrue signed at the same time after a year at City. We shared a flat in Dinas Powys, just past Penarth on the way to Barry Island, and it was a lovely place to live, then when Dave joined weeks later he stayed with us initially before he bought a house and John Lewis moved in with him. Dave had no reason to think his future wasn't at City. It was great for Cardiff to sign him; we had a number of young players making their way into the first-team squad and they included Tarki Micallef and Paul Giles. The side was struggling at the start of 1981/82, crowds were low and we had a few barriers to overcome, which included having two black brothers in the team. We began to get more supporters from diverse communities too as time went on.

As I didn't join Cardiff until mid-September, they'd already begun their Second Division season. It hadn't started too well either. We lost three out of the first four, with a draw at Oldham on the opening day. The previous season, 1980/81, had seen the Bluebirds avoid relegation on goal difference as Preston dropped into the Third Division. It didn't help that Swansea were promoted to the First Division and qualified for the UEFA Cup after they won the Welsh Cup. I really hoped I could add some spark and get us up the table as quickly as possible. I'd gone from crowds of 30,000-plus to under 10,000, so it was such a shift from Maine Road, Anfield, Old Trafford, and Wembley, of course.

In the week prior to my signing, Richie Morgan had kept supporters updated in the matchday programme of his transfer plans:

> In my office was Dave Bennett whose transfer I was trying to tie up from Manchester City while on the transatlantic telephone I was talking to Vancouver Whitecaps with the aim of landing Terry Yorath as our player-coach. Just before this frantic spurt of activity I had completed the signing of Dave's younger brother, Gary. I had also settled a loan deal with Preston to bring back Peter Sayer. I know that Cardiff City have been accused of lack of ambition. Well, these moves should nail that charge – believe me, there has never been anything wrong with Cardiff's ambition. I know that we have a side

short of two or three quality players and everyone at Ninian Park has been working hard to come up with the answers. Now we are on the way to solutions. Dave Bennett, a player who would still be playing at Maine Road but for the arrival of Trevor Francis, is a striker I have wanted for some while. But I was determined that the name should not come out – there have been too many false starts in the past. Our last two results emphasise once again the crossroads position of the current squad. It is good but not quite good enough. At the same time as I was talking with Dave Bennett, I was assessing the very real potential of Gary. He is a central defender of considerable promise and I think he will progress here.

My debut came at Oakwell, home of Barnsley, a week after we secured our first win of the season, 3-2 at Luton. Paul and I were drafted in alongside Gary Stevens, the three of us up front. Our tactics were positive, the defence coped well with everything thrown at them and after the Luton win it was the best week of the season so far. Gary Stevens' winner just after the hour sealed what was now three points for a win after it changed from two in the summer. It was around this time the Terry Yorath link ceased as he stayed at Vancouver Whitecaps, and we came back down to earth with a bump a week later as Newcastle came to South Wales.

My home debut coincided with a piece in the matchday programme:

> I'm very happy to be here. Joining Cardiff City has provided me with a special challenge. I think it is good for brothers to be in the same dressing room as when one does better than the other that provides motivation for the latter to make a special effort. That spirit can only help both of us to raise our performances. Last season was my best in football, naturally the cup final was a disappointment but there are a great many players in the country who would give anything to play at Wembley. I feel that my game is improving all the time and I'm really looking forward to starting all over again at Cardiff. There was no way that I was going to be satisfied with reserve team football after my performances last season. If I did well last season at Maine Road, I want to go one better here. I've a whole host of targets including a winner's medal at Wembley and playing for England. Of my two positions I think I prefer the scoring opportunities that playing up

front provide. This is the right challenge at the right time for me.

The crowd of 5,764 was a real eye-opener for me. Given Newcastle's renowned support, Ninian Park was more than half empty. It didn't help when Imre Varadi took home the match ball in their 4-0 win. Our first home win had to wait until 17 October, with my first goal in front of the Bluebirds' home support, but only about 4,000 were there to see it when we beat Bolton 2-1. This was the pattern throughout the season, and we were comfortably mid-table by the New Year, but five games without a goal in February/March saw us drop to 20th. From there on in it was a battle for us. We gave ourselves hope with three home wins on the bounce, one a 5-4 cracker with Cambridge. Away form saw only one win after September and that was the penultimate game of the season at fellow strugglers Grimsby.

Richie Morgan had departed after the struggle in February and Len Ashurst took over. His first game at Ninian Park was the Cambridge nine-goal thriller. We'd led 5-2 at half-time, Gary Stevens with a hat-trick, but even then we were hanging on for the final few minutes.

Len's man-management was excellent. The night before the Watford win in April I'd been out on the Friday to Bananas, a snooker club in Cardiff, with Gary and Tarki.

We were meant to leave by seven, but the night rolled on and soon it was ten. As we walked out the chairman walked past. I had a fitness test at 10am, five hours before the game, and scored in our 2-0 win. A week later Len called the three of us into his office and said to drink vodka and orange, so it wasn't obvious we were having a drink. There was trust, and in return you wanted to repay him.

The goals dried up in May against fellow strugglers Derby and Crystal Palace. Luton were already champions when they came to Ninian Park on the final day of our season, a Monday night. The fixture was originally scheduled for Wednesday, 5 May but it was postponed, so it was now a must-win, literally, to send Bolton down and keep us up. Luton were well organised and deserved their promotion, no doubt the best team in the division. Our immediate future hinged on the three points and the 10,000 packed into the ground. We needed them, and it was a real boost to see the stadium so full. But it wasn't to be on a night that was mirrored throughout the season – we just weren't good enough. Luton won 3-2 and it would be the Third Division for us in 1982/83. I finished the season with seven goals in 42 appearances.

The bookmakers made us 10/1 second favourites behind Sheffield United for promotion back to the Second Division. We knew we'd get less time on the ball in the

Third Division and that sides would close us down quicker. They'd be physical, and we'd have to earn the right to play. Len, and Jimmy Mullen, our captain, knew the division well and set about transforming the squad in the summer of 1982.

In our clashes with Cambridge United the previous season they'd given us two close games; they had a tight-knit squad with good players. Midfielder Roger Gibbins had scored against us in both games, breaking into the box, timing his runs, and he recalls his move to Cardiff:

> John Docherty called me into his office, and it was totally unexpected when he told me I could leave Cambridge. The club couldn't afford us all. In 1982 the rules changed on gate receipts where before the money was divided equally between home and away clubs. It was altered so that only the home sides got the money and we had crowds of 4,000 at the Abbey Stadium. We'd gone from sharing the money for an away trip to West Ham or Newcastle to receiving nothing and having to cover the cost of a hotel stay ourselves on the longer trips. A scout based in Cambridge, Paddy Southam, recommended me to Len and we drove down to meet him at Ninian Park. Len had never even seen me play and said he was looking to

build as they'd just been relegated. I would be his No.8 in a 4-4-2, the central midfielder who'd get into the danger areas and capitalise on the chances we created.

When Roger signed, we only had nine players under contract. The core was there: Andy Dibble, Linden Jones, Gary and me. During that summer we were joined by Jeff Hemmerman, Dave Tong and Paul Bodin. We had a reliable, hard-working squad of 14/15 professionals, with younger players Paul Maddy and Paul Giles on the verge of breaking through. Gary Stevens, our top scorer the previous season, had left us short up front with his departure as we prepared to face Wrexham on the opening day. His 18 goals, 13 in the league, would need to be replaced. Paul Sugrue also left to join Middlesbrough after fewer than ten appearances all season. We'd been to St Athan pre-season, down in South Wales, and we all bonded doing the assault courses and built up a real camaraderie. There was a belief among us as we went into the season.

Wrexham had been relegated alongside us and Orient. We'd all struggled away from home and simply not scored enough. Len's recruitment had gone well, although our pre-season saw two defeats in the five games. Our 2-1 defeat would prove to be our only home loss of the season and Wrexham's only win on their travels. An opening-day defeat was commonplace in those days, as you've had eight weeks off and not done too much before pre-season, which is all about getting fit again. You'd have had a good holiday during the summer; some would have a complete break and then do a bit of running in preparation for the return. The squad got on well from the outset and we were confident of a good start, so were disappointed with the loss to Wrexham.

A week later we travelled to Millwall and won 4-0. I'd scored in both games. We ran out the tunnel at Millwall and their fans pelted stuff at us, but it was one of our best games of the season. I remember coming away from the ground thinking this could be the start of something. However, football being football, early injuries then hampered us, John Lewis especially, after his performance at Millwall, as Orient thumped us 4-0 at Brisbane Road. The lack of squad depth hit us unexpectedly. John gave us such a good balance and we really missed him that day.

Len added to the squad with the signing of Billy Woof, a No.9, who joined from Blyth Spartans on a short-term deal – three days. We trailed 2-1 at home to Wigan before Gary equalised and then Billy scored an 86th-minute winner. His time in South Wales ended almost as soon as it started as he fell out with Len after the game and we never saw him again. Billy got in his car and drove back up north, later signing for Hull.

Wins against Walsall, Sheffield United and Exeter left us in third position as we moved into October. Jeff Hemmerman had scored in four successive games. We all felt we weren't pulling up any trees and should have been. A key moment occurred after a meeting between the senior professionals and involved me. Roger takes on the story:

> I got on great with Dave from the start. He was bubbly, confident and there was something about him that kept the atmosphere going – he was great for the dressing room. When I signed, I was in digs for three months and we bonded well. I liked to go out, as did Dave and Gary, which was nothing unusual in those days. Dave would be seen out by the chairman on many occasions, but he'd turn a blind eye because he did so well for us. I never went out on a Thursday or Friday before a game, I stuck to the rules. You had to wind down and relax, although I didn't take it to midnight on the Friday like Dave and Gary. Len made it a rule that we were not allowed out in Cardiff, so Dave and Gary went over to Bristol instead. You could mix with the fans, there was no social media and

people weren't out to get a photo with you. As a player he was brilliant, and Cardiff was good for him. Len knew our strengths and weaknesses; if we stopped producing, he'd step in and have a word. He would protect us and knew we were out and about, but it made you want to perform to your best for him, which we did.

We had a little committee, Jimmy Mullen, Phil Dwyer and me, that used to see Len every now and again. Len would ask how the boys were and how the dressing room was. We'd had one of these meetings and all agreed we weren't happy with Dave. We knew how good he was, but he was killing us defensively, doing his stuff but then not getting back into position and teams were overloading Linden Jones, our right-back. Len told us to sort it, to which we all baulked and then realised he did actually want us to talk to Dave! We called a players' meeting in the dressing room and Jimmy spoke to Dave to say we needed more from him; we didn't expect him to tackle and win 50/50s but we needed him to make up the four in midfield and support Linden. He was a bit taken aback initially but he took it on board, and he did it. I think it made him an even better player. This was one of the best seasons of my career. I'd tell Dave he was our star man but he'd get the job done. When he moved to Coventry, he had Brian Borrows on the right side and you could see how well they worked together over the years. Our team's mantra was 'if you lose the ball, switch on and get it back'. Teams couldn't handle us.

The win over Sheffield United saw Godfrey Ingram's debut in front of the home crowd. We'd signed him from San Jose Earthquakes in the US. Bob Grogan paid in instalments; the first £20,000 secured the deal and the fee was in the region of £200,000. We thought nothing more of it until two months later when he returned to San Jose. Godfrey did have family in South Wales, and he went on to play for many years in the US indoor league. He lived in a bed and breakfast in Penarth and there was a real flair about his play.

October saw us consolidate in fourth place. We still weren't pulling up any trees, but we were there or thereabouts. Bournemouth and Huddersfield were always difficult away games and proved so, especially at Leeds Road when Mark Lillis scored all four for them. Our form at Ninian Park was good, wins over Gillingham, Bradford and Portsmouth keeping up the pressure on the leaders.

Goalkeeping proved to be a problem throughout the season, not the quality, just the injuries and misfortune. Andy Dibble, just 17, was brilliant but he got injured early on and Martin Thomas came in on loan for part of the season. Dibs lived in Cwmbran and used to train then bus it each day as he was too young to drive. Wins at Reading and then at home to Preston took us into second place and it was all knitting together nicely. Then we travelled to Sincil Bank, home of Lincoln, and the wheels temporarily came off.

Colin Murphy was in charge at Lincoln, who were a side in the mould of Cambridge under John Beck a few years later. In the Lincoln side that November afternoon was Trevor Peake, who'd become a team-mate of mine within a year. Trevor remembers Cardiff's visit to Lincoln:

> Colin would play little games with the opposition. Away teams would find their dressing room floor wet through, with the windows wide open and heating turned off. Sincil Bank was a spartan little ground, just over 6,000 were there that day; it holds just over ten. Dave had given Cardiff a half-time lead, but the game turned before the hour when Marshall Burke, our midfielder, clattered him and he retaliated. The ref waved the red card and Dave was off. We turned the game

on its head and won 2-1. Paul Bodin's own goal clinched the points for us. It was the only time Dave was sent off in his career.

Roger remembered it well:

> It wasn't a good day at Lincoln. Dave had put us into the lead, we were in control. The ground was very open, and the wind howled across the pitch. He was man-marked throughout; they knew he was our catalyst. They'd tried to get one in on him early and it hadn't knocked him out of his stride. If you don't succeed, try again, almost.

I remember it well too! Marshall Burke went over the top and I retaliated. I tried to grab him because he was out of order. We were 1-0 up, I was playing well and had scored. Lincoln sat top of the league, we were in second, they were clear by eight points and had won all seven home games. I apologised to the lads afterwards as we were chasing them down at the top of the table. I learned my lesson and it never happened again. I picked up a two-match ban as a result. In those days you had to look after yourself on the pitch, as the tackle from behind was commonplace and it was a very fiery environment. It was a straight red too, but moving forwards from that moment I was able to foresee trouble and ensured I didn't let myself or my team-mates down again.

The FA Cup first round gave us a banana skin tie at Wokingham Town, who'd progressed through five rounds and eight matches. They were part-time and their main striker, George Torrance, was a soldier in the British Army, recently posted to Berlin for two years. He was flown back to play in the game, a sell-out, and after 15 minutes he scored. The place went mad. We took the tie to a replay, eventually equalising through David Tong, but it was a difficult game on a cold, dark day, a typical cup tie. Three days later we won the replay 3-0 in Godfrey's last game for us; he scored too. San Jose wanted to take him back to the States. They paid us the deposit we'd paid in the first place and then Len brought Bob Hatton to the club as his replacement, a masterstroke. Sheffield United's manager Ian Porterfield was managed by Len while he was at Sheffield Wednesday and it showed his respect for him as we had the first refusal on Bob.

Bob was 35 at the time, fresh from promotion with Sheffield United. On his first appearance at Ninian Park he scored after three minutes, although it couldn't prevent a draw with Chesterfield off the back of a draw at Doncaster. His signing bolstered our options in attack, but he always had time on the ball. We were in fourth place with the top three guaranteed promotion, no play-offs in those days. It was key we maintained our form as Weymouth visited for the FA Cup second-round tie. We had three big games approaching Christmas to set ourselves up for the New Year and a real push for promotion.

At half-time it was all going to plan. We'd settled, scored two in quick succession on the half-hour but we hadn't taken them lightly, far from it. Roger and Jeff had scored, and we came out for the second half thinking one more will seal victory. They had nothing to lose, and whether we took our foot off the gas or not, I'm not sure, but Weymouth upped their game and went for it. We gave away a sloppy goal before the hour and lost momentum. Their Italian waiter scored, Anni Iannone, then two goals in the last ten minutes and we couldn't force a replay. The headlines were horrendous the next day. We'd missed out on the third-round draw, which was such a disappointment for us and the fans. There was no weakened team either as you just didn't do that. You played your strongest side. You didn't rotate anyone, you simply didn't have the squad numbers to do so. Weymouth were knocked out in the third round at Cambridge United, as so often happens; the smaller side causes the upset then bows out at the next hurdle.

On the Monday morning, Len wheeled out the television and the VHS recorder. We'd never done that kind of thing before, and it was so uncomfortable watching the whole game, a really horrible experience. But it did the trick. A few fingers were pointed and we went on to a tricky Friday night game down at Southend, who, along with Tranmere, often played on a Friday night so they could draw from the big clubs' fanbase locally. It was cold and wet; the mist was rising and Roger's late winner along with another from Bob Hatton took us second as we went into Christmas. We started to turn negatives into positives. Hindsight is great – would our season have been any different if we hadn't lost to Weymouth?

Unusually for December we didn't have a game for ten days, including Boxing Day. It gave us a chance to rest up, clear the niggles and look to the next game. You might be tired at times, but we all wanted to play, as you might not get back in the side if you had a rest. It was still one substitute in those days, and you could rely on the matchday programme to list the correct starting XI. It was No.1 to No.11 and that side would consistently be the line-up unless injury intervened. That season eight of us played 35 games or more, and the back four picked itself: Linden, Gary, Jimmy and Phil, with Dave Tong, Roger and me in the midfield, John Lewis on the left, with Bob and Jeff up front. Tarki played up front before Bob arrived, Paul Giles would play if one of the wingers was out, Paul Maddy in midfield likewise.

OFF TO THE VALLEYS

After ten days' break it was two games in two days, which was usual then. The fixtures computer didn't always show common sense; however, in 1982/83 it was switched on. Newport at home followed a day later with a trip down the M5 to Plymouth, then Bristol Rovers at home on New Year's Day. We took nine points out of nine before a trip to Brentford and Stan Bowles. Stan opened the scoring before Roger and Jeff with a brace gave us three more points. Jeff scored six over the festive period as the crowds soared. Over 15,000 for Newport's visit and then nearly 11,000 for Bristol Rovers. We were second, playing superbly and even had Clive Thomas referee the South Wales derby with Newport, a consideration to the officials at Christmas time too, as he lived in Porthcawl.

With no FA Cup third round for us, our unbeaten run continued with a point at Wrexham then wins over Walsall and Exeter before we topped the table with victory at home to Millwall, when both Gary and I scored. We were flying and hadn't lost since Weymouth, until we visited Bramall Lane. Always a difficult place to visit, a passionate, loyal crowd, we lost 2-0 but we were in a fantastic position with 18 games remaining. Len didn't get too excited when things were going well, and he wasn't too down if we slipped up. A real thinker, he knew his squad was good enough, and if you've done well consistently throughout the season then you're going to have one or two mishaps. He also couldn't make many changes even if he wanted to as we didn't have the personnel. We knew we were good enough and bounced back with a thumping of Oxford when Len picked up January's manager of the month award, a gallon bottle of Bell's Whisky.

Around this time, due to suspensions and injuries, Len had tried to add a couple of loanees, Lou Macari and Trevor Brooking. Macari was out of favour at Manchester United, while Brooking was on the comeback after a long-standing groin injury that impacted his involvement in the 1982 World Cup. He'd only played once that season and Len hoped to bring him in, but it didn't happen.

The goalkeeping position was unlike any I've known during my career. After Dibs' injury, Martin Thomas came in on loan from Bristol Rovers. Dibs then returned and featured in our trip to Bradford on a Wednesday night up in Yorkshire. It didn't go well. He was carried off in the first half with damaged knee ligaments on a night when we lost top spot to Portsmouth and didn't quite play like we knew we could. With only one substitute we used both Phil Dwyer and Linden Jones in goal. Dibs wouldn't return until mid-April. Bradford were always a strong side at Valley Parade and proved so again in their 4-2 win.

The loan system was used extensively by Len, as we simply didn't have the money to buy players. We later found out we'd used more loan players during the season than any other team in the Football League. Only two of the squad were under 20 – experience was key for Len.

Our consistency had been our strength, and this was epitomised by David Tong in our midfield. He'd signed in the summer from Shrewsbury and moved down, while his family stayed put until they sold their house. Along with Roger and John Lewis, the midfield was the most settled part of the side and each one of them brought something different. The top four, Portsmouth, ourselves, Lincoln and Huddersfield, were invincible at home, but it would be our away form that would make the difference. They all possessed a 20-goal-a-season player, in Pompey's case, two. Lincoln had Derek Bell, while Mark Lillis, as we well know, was prolific for Huddersfield.

For the visit of Bournemouth, Len brought in Jim Brown as cover for Dibs. Jim had spent the previous three years in the US playing for Detroit Express in the NASL. His team-mates included Trevor Francis and Ted MacDougall, and they'd later sign several Coventry players, including Mark Hateley and Gary Bannister. Jim played three times for us on loan before Len brought in Watford's Eric Steele, in later years part of Manchester United's backroom staff. Bournemouth battled well for a point before a tricky trip to Gillingham was navigated with a 3-2 win. We were holding second spot going into March and drew three successive matches. The trip to Portsmouth was something else. Over 4,000 fans made the trip and there were 24,000 in Fratton Park for first versus second. Pompey had Billy Rafferty and Alan Biley close to 20 goals each, so to keep a clean sheet that day we did well. City fans broke the clock, if I remember rightly. It's a great ground, full of atmosphere and close to the fans.

After a poor defeat to Preston, Lincoln came to Ninian Park, with memories of our defeat and my red card in the reverse fixture. The trouble during and after that away game has been well documented. Cardiff fans invaded the home seats and then it all spilled on to the pitch after we'd lost. Lincoln had a decent side, with my old mate Trevor Peake, who we'll hear from in due course, Glenn Cockerill and Gordon Hobson, who both moved to Southampton. They looked a good bet for automatic promotion. Thankfully, this time Gary's goal won it for us. We knew the chasing pack were after us, with Newport scoring goals for fun. Three points for a win, though, was making a difference. In close games it was massive to nick a win, which we did against Lincoln. Eric Steele had added further experience to the defence and, with Dibs still to return, his signing had proved wise.

Every game was huge at this point. A lot of the time you get two or three teams close together but here you had five or six. Another draw at home to Plymouth took us to the clash of the season at Somerton Park, Newport. County had Tommy Tynan and John Aldridge, who were a lower league match for anyone. They'd won six out of seven and could go top if they beat us. Results around us were wrecking pools coupons, with the unpredictability of the matches. Our Easter Monday clash kicked off at 11am and would prove to be a real turning point in our season.

I didn't play that day, as I was injured against Reading. Newport's side was strong and there were 16,000 there. We even had a First Division referee, Ray Lewis. Their average home crowd for the season was 5,000. The build-up to the game and early kick-off gave it a little bit of extra spice. John Aldridge scored the only goal; our dressing room was silent afterwards. Gary had a goal disallowed, which didn't help matters. We dropped to fourth as Newport went top, and they were flying.

Len gave us two choices after the game, as we hadn't played that badly: 'Either let it all slide or we pick ourselves up and get going again.' Newport didn't win another game and we were unbeaten in the final seven matches … it's a funny old game. This was a key turning point after Weymouth, and we responded in a similar fashion both times.

Cardiff hadn't had much to shout about in recent seasons. Swansea had moved through the divisions under John Toshack and were in the First Division, while rugby union was massive in South Wales. Finally, football was about to take off. A group of players who worked for each other, put their foot in, players who could play. Bob Hatton was just fantastic for us, what a signing. Len had brought Frank Burrows in with him, as they could see the potential and he added to it. With seven games to play we regrouped and got ourselves prepared for the visit of relegation-bound Doncaster Rovers.

In the build-up to the game the PFA held its awards dinner. Now bear in mind we were fourth, had scored over 60 goals and conceded just 12 in 20 home games. Not one Cardiff City player made the team of the year. Those who were nominated included Trevor Peake, Steve Bruce, Micky Adams, Neil Webb, Glenn Cockerill, Kerry Dixon and Alan Biley. Before his injury, Andy Dibble was outstanding, Jeff and Bob were scoring for fun, Gary and myself didn't do too badly either. In those days you might have only played against a player once and had to rely on gossip and the highlights if featured on *The Big Match*. There wasn't the widespread 24/7 features available nowadays.

Doncaster had struggled most of the season, but it was one of those that you just couldn't take for granted. Dave

Tong and Roger put us two up early on and the game was over as a contest. It was Eric Steele's last game for us before Dibs returned for the draw at Wigan. Gary saw red for two yellow cards, a one-match ban for the Chesterfield away day. It set us up nicely for Southend's visit. They were mid-table and safe; we were still in fourth but only two points off leaders Huddersfield. Bristol Rovers had put themselves back in the hunt and Portsmouth had thumped Newport 3-0 away from home. We were four up just after half-time. Two from John Lewis among the goals, and it set us up nicely for the trip to bottom side Chesterfield.

What's difficult to manage in a small squad is suspensions. One is okay, two is a challenge but three is a real dent in the numbers. Gary, Linden and Phil were all suspended, and only Jimmy Mullen from the usual back four was fit. Roger dropped to centre-half, while Paul Bodin and John Lewis covered the full-back positions. Paul Maddy and Paul Giles showed their quality again, and they all contributed to our success. I remember our fans lifting Roger on to their shoulders after our 1-0 win. My goal gave us the three points and kept the pressure on, but it was another clean sheet for us and a real squad effort that day. The three of them back from suspension gave us a further lift for Brentford's visit on Easter Monday. Ninian Park started to see bigger attendances, and the momentum and feel-good factor was around the city with 9,000 packed into Ninian Park with three games to go.

Brentford's side were full of goals, with Keith Cassells and Stan Bowles, while their midfield was as tough as they come: Terry Hurlock and Chris Kamara. At this stage we just had to focus on our own games and not worry about what was going on elsewhere. Our 3-1 win took us into second place as Bob scored what would turn out to be his last career goal, along with one for myself and an own goal. The momentum was clear to see, and crowds were flocking to Ninian Park. It was now ours to lose, along with leaders Portsmouth, for whom Alan Biley just couldn't miss. Huddersfield's away form had hindered them, along with a waterlogged pitch postponement against Wigan ... in early May. Sat in third place, their next game saw Newport visit Leeds Road, with Huddersfield unbeaten at home all season, and that record would continue.

It was 7 May 1983, the day Cardiff City were promoted back to the Second Division. Newport lost at Huddersfield and our 2-0 win in front of over 11,000 fans saw the good times roll back into Cardiff. We played well that day. The pressure was on and we turned on the style. John Lewis and I sealed the three points. Looking back now it was an Orient side languishing in the lower half of the table, yet they had Mervyn Day in goal, Barry Silkman, Colin Foster, later of Forest, and the No.9 was a certain Keith Houchen. There was scope for an upset, but Len prepared us well, kept us calm and the biggest crowd of the season roared us on. Often on the big occasion you can trip up, but that day was a good one, 'a fine win' as Len put it. We'd won 17 of our 23 home games and lost just the once, on the opening day to Wrexham. You don't get many seasons like this, and it's only after the event you realise what an achievement it was and just how good that small group of players was.

The celebrations began as soon as the final whistle blew. We were all up in the directors' box, Len and Jimmy Goodfellow saluting the fans with a bottle of champagne. They'd all run on to the pitch and surrounded the tunnel area. The Orient goal was my favourite of that season purely because of the importance, coming when it mattered, and we were able to secure the goal we'd set out to achieve back in August.

Our final game was at Eastville, the old home of Bristol Rovers. They had Alan Ball in their midfield at the end of his career and were led by Bobby Gould. Unbeknown to us, Bobby wasn't at the game. A story had found its way into the papers linking him with the Coventry job, even though Dave Sexton was still in charge there. Rovers' chairman had told him to stay away. Their home record was one of the best, but they'd slipped up away from home and tailed away in the last few games.

Roger opened the scoring in typical fashion, arriving in the penalty area and finishing with aplomb. The pressure was off, and we were playing well until just before half-time when the stuffing was knocked out of us. Jeff moved in towards goal and Phil Kite, Rovers' keeper, dived at his feet. Jeff hardly moved. He was carried off just before half-time and we walked into the dressing room to find him laid out on the bench. Everyone was really upset; we were tight-knit and it was like letting the air out of a balloon. I know that Phil Kite joined Cardiff after I left and told Roger how terrible he felt at the knee injury Jeff suffered. He was 28 or 29 at the time, Jeff, and it took him a year to return, but he couldn't regain his fitness and retired soon after. Cardiff arranged a testimonial for him against Aston Villa in 1984. Ironically, he's run a physiotherapy practice in Newport ever since.

We ended up drawing 1-1 on the final day, Nicky Platnauer levelling for Rovers. He'd soon be a team-mate of mine and played for Cardiff in later years. Portsmouth went up as champions, five points clear of us as we totalled 86 points. In total we won 25 games and scored 76 times. Huddersfield took the third promotion spot as Newport's slump after beating us saw them four points off the pace. Oxford, Lincoln and Bristol Rovers followed them. Reading went down despite having Kerry Dixon in their side, along with Wrexham, Doncaster and Chesterfield. Little did I know that it wasn't just a new season that was ahead for me, there was also a transfer that would define the rest of my career, bringing with it final-day relegation battles, team spirit like I'd never known before and another crack at Wembley glory.

4
Sky-High Blues

ONCE THE season with Cardiff had ended, Bob Hatton announced his retirement, Jeff was in rehab for his knee injury and I was attracting interest from clubs, including Arsenal and Coventry. Bobby Gould used to scout over at Ninian Park from his base in the north Somerset area and had just taken over at his hometown club, Coventry City, replacing Dave Sexton:

> Ninian Park was an easy journey for me, and I'd watch many games there. Dave was always one player in the back of my mind, so when I got the Coventry job he was in my top three transfer targets that I had to go out and buy. The other two were Nicky Platnauer and Graham Withey over at Bristol Rovers. I just felt they all had a hunger to want to be successful, they wanted to

go forward in their careers. They all suited me down to the ground.

What impressed me with Dave was the way he kept his heels white, not like the players of today who come inside at every opportunity. It's an expression Ron Greenwood told me about when I played for West Ham, keeping the width and making sure your players in the wide positions hold their position and give you as much opportunity to attack the full-back as possible. You can see what's coming at you if you hold your position. If the full-back rushes in you can play it round the back of him into the space; if he's not committing you can take a touch and look up. I wanted natural width in my Coventry side because as a centre-forward I wanted that and had Willie Humphries and Ronnie Rees supply me. Dave was a cheeky chappie, but I thought, *You'll do for me.* He was a bit jack the lad but that was part of his make-up and he never let me down.

I'd always enjoyed playing at Coventry. They had good young players so I thought it would be a good move. It wasn't until I was on my way to Coventry that other clubs had come in for me. But I was excited at the prospect of playing with these young players at Coventry. Arsenal were in for me as well but couldn't get hold of me in the close season, as there were no mobile phones then. I was like the Scarlet Pimpernel, all over the place. Bobby tracked me down, the fee was £125,000 and I signed. I didn't find out about Arsenal's interest until a little bit later on. They ended up signing Brian Marwood because they'd been looking for a right-sided winger, so they signed him. As I was moving up to the First Division, Manchester City had been relegated on the last day of 1982/83, with Raddy Antic's late winner at Maine Road ensuring Luton's survival, while City dropped into the Second Division.

The fixture list had already been produced prior to me leaving Cardiff and our first home game was, you've guessed it, Manchester City, now under Billy McNeill's management.

I loved my two years in Cardiff. The goal I scored against Orient was my favourite, probably because of the importance, sealing promotion and seeing how happy it made the fans. It was a great season to be involved in. Promotion campaigns, like all seasons, are like a marathon, you've just got to keep going, win the battles and then let your quality take over, and we had that in abundance. With me leaving, it would also be the first time in a number of years that Gary and I were not at the same club:

Dave was one of the outstanding players in the division, there were always people there to watch him, but credit to Coventry who were in the process of building a new team. They had lost the bulk of their 1982/83 side when they allowed their contracts to run out and they moved far and wide. Dave Sexton had been sacked and Bobby Gould brought in, who was managing in the First Division for the first time. Bobby saw the role that Dave could play; slowly but surely he began to build a squad in pre-season. When Dave left the focus switched to me and how I would manage without him in the side. People would say I didn't realise he was that good, but I did, it was a big loss for us along with Bob Hatton and Jeff Hemmerman.

Reading the praise of Len Ashurst for both Gary and me was quite humbling:

> Dave turned many a game our way during the season with a bit of magic on the ball. At this level he can do things no other players can, and he has the ability to win matches off his own bat. His telling crosses have created many goals

for Bob and Jeff and he was the best winger in the division, no doubt about that. Not since the Charles brothers, John and Mel, have Cardiff had such a popular double act. Gary's pace, control and goalscoring ability make him the most exciting defender in the Third Division. There's no limit to what he could achieve. I know where I could sell him for a good fee tomorrow if I wanted to.

The extra responsibility helped me too. People looked to me to do something special and make things happen and I thrived on that. At Manchester City I, more often than not, gave the ball to a big-name player, play the way you're facing, don't take too many risks. Playing in the Third Division was very hard physically and I took my fair share of whacks from full-backs.

When I joined Coventry it was just before my birthday, early July, and as we all know there was a big exodus of excellent young players after the 1982/83 season. Mark Hateley, Les Sealey, Danny Thomas, Gary Gillespie, Steve Whitton and Paul Dyson, alongside the more experienced Gerry Francis and Jim Melrose. Also Garry Thompson had been sold in the spring to West Brom, Jimmy Hill sanctioning the sale for much-needed funds. Coventry had lads like Danny Thomas, Thompson and Tommy English, all roughly the same age as me, who I knew of because I'd played against them in the Central League. I thought they were good players and that would be a good move for me. Obviously, I signed and then they all left! That was a little bit disappointing. It was just another challenge.

Bobby was very enthusiastic. I knew of Bobby Gould because I'd played against his Bristol Rovers side while I was at Cardiff. Bobby knew what I could offer. My first impressions of Bobby were that he was enthusiastic, he wanted to win and he had his own style. He was a little bit off the wall, he was a little bit erratic with some things but that was the manager he was and that was the character of the man. He came into the club with new ideas and ambition. He was a local lad and wanted to take the club places. He wanted to do things his way and if certain players weren't part of that then he'd move them on quick. Some of the older players might have been wondering what was going on. Myself, I always got on well with Bobby. He always played me so I haven't got a bad word to say against him. I might not have always agreed with his tactics but that's football, that's football management, you try things sometimes and they don't work. Maybe he could have listened to the older players a little bit and learned from them but that was who he was.

Bobby's biggest task when I arrived was to put a squad together. There weren't many players left for him to work with when he arrived: Brian Roberts, Steve Jacobs, Steve Hunt and Gerry Daly were first-team regulars, but the rest of the squad were young lads like Lloyd McGrath, John Hendrie, Peter Hormantschuk, Ian Butterworth and Martin Singleton, with minimal first-team games so far. The fans were disenchanted with the summer activity, and we hoped we could win them round. Talbot ended their sponsorship and we watched George Curtis drive up to Luton to retrieve Les Sealey's car as he'd taken it to Luton with him.

Transfer activity was slow as we moved closer to the start of the season. Our first game wasn't until 27 August at Watford, unlike nowadays with the first week in August, so there was time for Bobby to recruit. Dave Bamber had signed from Blackpool, a big No.9, and he was quickly followed by Trevor Peake, one of Lincoln's central defenders the previous season. Left-back Micky Adams and experienced defender Sam Allardyce soon joined, but as we moved into August the squad was still threadbare. He'd tried to sign more experienced players, but the club just couldn't afford them. Kenny Burns was one. Charlie George had been a team-mate of Bobby's at Arsenal and he was on trial through the summer but couldn't shake off the injuries he'd picked up during his career. Bristol Rovers' Nicky Platnauer and Graham Withey I'd played against for Cardiff in my final game, and we knew Bobby was keen to bring them to the club. They signed along with Ashley Grimes, who'd been at Manchester United through their youth system but had struggled to find regular game time. We also needed an experienced goalkeeper, as Tim Dalton and Perry Suckling were teenagers, and only Perry had played in the first team, so Raddy Avramovic, with over 150 appearances for Notts County, joined as our new No.1 to replace Les Sealey.

One of our pre-season friendlies saw us travel to Benfica for a 2-2 draw. Tim Dalton, an Irish lad, was in goal that day at the famous Stadium of Light. How Bobby got that fixture in place we'll never know but it was a real coup and we played well. The bookies tipped us for relegation, which was no real surprise given the fact we were in the middle of a huge rebuild, but this only inspired us all with points to prove and new challenges across the team. After our Portugal trip we were brought back down to earth with a week in Bridlington, with friendlies pencilled in.

At the same time as I was making my debut for Manchester City, a small, pacy striker was making people sit up and take notice over at Tottenham. Trevor Gould, Bobby's brother, had seen Terry Gibson in action and recommended him. The next morning Terry was in Coventry for talks. Bear in mind there was now a week until the season began, and Terry was given 15 minutes to decide if he wanted to sign as we needed a centre-forward to partner Dave Bamber. Terry's wife, Paula, found out he'd left Tottenham when she turned on the London sports news, as he hadn't arrived home from the Midlands yet and had no way of telling her. We had eight or nine players out training the day he arrived. Fortunately for us a three-year contract on £300 a week was duly signed with a promise of first-team football. In those days the medical consisted of a urine test and blood pressure check; how times have changed.

All the new arrivals stayed at the Post House hotel in Walsgrave, and we had almost the whole team there. We'd all eat our evening meal together, it was like being in the club, the bonding and camaraderie. Everyone there was looking for a place to live at a new club and it brought us all together. One man we hadn't met yet was midfielder Michael Gynn, who'd signed late on 26 August with the Watford game kicking off at 3pm the next day. The first we saw of Gynny was when he walked into the pre-match hotel after driving from Peterborough that morning. We're sat there with our tea and toast and in he walked. He had a blinder that day too. I'd picked up an injury so wouldn't make my debut until the sixth game, at home to Leicester, but we were all together at the games and got off to a great start with a 3-2 win at Vicarage Road. Terry scored on his debut, along with two own goals against a Graham Taylor-managed Watford, who were fresh from finishing runners-up to Liverpool the previous season.

Three days later we're at White Hart Lane facing Hoddle, Clemence, Archibald and Brazil, with Danny Thomas in their side. With ten minutes remaining debutant Graham Withey fired home at the back post and we've taken another point, with over 35,000 there and the opening home game against Everton to follow. Howard Kendall had signed Trevor Steven from Burnley and he had a terrific game on the right side of midfield. We all know what he achieved in seasons to come but Everton were just getting going on the path to glories, and Sheedy fired in a rocket to level the game.

With so many of us from outside the city, we trained on the Tuesday and then had Wednesday off, so everyone cleared off back home, with us all living in the Post House, and then returned on Thursday. Gibbo would meet Perry Suckling and Steve Jacobs at Watford Gap for breakfast, and they'd drive up. Sam was commuting from Bolton, myself from Manchester along with Ashley Grimes, while Trevor Peake was one of the few home-based players, up in Nuneaton. It was hard to settle initially for a few of the London lads, especially as this was before the M25 opened. We didn't know much about each other, apart from those we'd played against, but it was good fun and a great dressing room to be a part of. We used to play a lot of cards of an evening as we had to behave. Gibbo brought his dog up from London to stay at the hotel while he was waiting to move into Les Sealey's old house. Les was married to Terry's cousin, Elaine. Eventually, I moved to Nuneaton, and Trevor would pick me up for training every day and ferry me around. He'd always want to get home quick, while I'd be chatting to someone. I could hear him revving the engine and sounding the horn.

The Sky Blue Connexion was a fantastic base for us. It was a couple of years old when I signed. The facilities were second to none as part of Jimmy Hill's vision, with two training pitches, an all-weather surface and indoor courts for both football and other sports. There was also a canteen where we all ate after training. Our venue was ahead of its time and not many clubs could boast such fabulous training grounds with such choice.

After recovering from a pre-season injury, I was on the bench for Leicester's visit to Highfield Road. On the back of our first defeat of the season at West Ham it was important to build on the early season momentum and bounce back.

Steve Whitton had smashed in a couple of trademark shots past Perry as the Hammers recovered from two early goals to win 5-2 and maintain their 100 per cent record, as they won their first five matches – and Ray Stewart missed a penalty, a rarity as we all knew how good he was. Leicester, managed by Gordon Milne, had been promoted from the Second Division and lost their first six games (they would stay up). Raddy made his first appearance for us, and it was great to finally get on the pitch when I replaced Keith Thompson. Our 2-1 win took us up to sixth before a run of three defeats in four saw us consolidate in mid-table.

Big Dave Bamber had missed a fair chunk of the season with illness, and he was in and out of hospital until finally they took his wisdom teeth out, thinking it would solve the problem. It didn't. He was still ill and eventually athlete's foot was found to be the cause of the blood infection. At Highbury he was inspired. Along with the winning goal, he was up against David O'Leary and Chris Whyte, and scored past Pat Jennings. For me I was back in the First Division, playing at the best grounds against the best players in the country.

One of those was Cyrille Regis, who scored in West Bromwich Albion's win at Highfield Road. We hadn't seen much of Micky Gynn since the opening-day win at Watford, but his return coincided with a nine-match unbeaten run. It was never dull at Coventry, and this took us up to fourth place. We were defying everyone, and during this run I collected the only yellow card of my career in our win at Birmingham. I can recall Sam Allardyce up against Mick Harford, a real powerhouse duel, and Mick went to hospital, which didn't happen often.

One of the highlights was a 4-2 win at Luton when I fired past Les from range. Kenilworth Road was always a cracking atmosphere, and that day was no exception. Bobby had been up to his tricks again in the transfer market when he treated his wife, Marge, to a night out in Yeovil, watching Wealdstone's left-back, Stuart Pearce, in action. He signed, trained on the Friday then put in a man-of-the-match performance against QPR the next day with his taped-up Puma Kings. What a player he was, and subsequently became, for us, Forest and England. He was a character straight away. He had a hell of a shot on him. My first impression of him was he was a very powerful defender. He was a typical London guy, very sure of himself. He was part of this huge turnover of players that we had around that time. We had so many players coming in and out over a year or so. I came up against him in training, him being a left-back and me being a right-winger. I enjoyed that. I always get asked about the hardest player I played against and in those days you were up against left-backs who were allowed to tackle from behind, they were allowed a free tackle against you. When you played against Stuart Pearce he always liked you to know he was there and that was whether it was in a game or just in training. You came up against him and you knew what he was going to do. You had to look after yourself and I had to let him know I was there.

I'd look at the fixtures and go, 'Okay, this next run of games will be Bailey, Dicks, Van den Hauwe, Kenny Sansom, Pearce,' all left-backs that were quick and would kick! I had to learn very quickly how to play against these players or I wasn't going to survive. I'd make them know I was there in more ways than one, whether dribbling past them or getting in first with a tackle. As a winger, if you were causing problems, the manager would give the word out for the defender to let the attacker know that they're there. I took some punishment. You had to show some character. If you let someone just keep on kicking you, then they're not going to stop kicking you.

Anyway, back to Stuart Pearce; his fifth game for us saw him marking Sammy Lee as reigning champions Liverpool and the *Match of the Day* cameras came to town. For the fans there was always the excitement of being on *Match of the Day* that evening, although Coventry weren't regulars by any means, so to see the trucks parked up as you arrived at the ground gave an extra edge, not least when John Motson walked into the ground as you knew the nation would be watching. Given the fact it was Liverpool, with all their star internationals, you also didn't want a thumping defeat in front of the watching millions.

By 4.45pm we'd moved into fourth place in the First Division. There were 21,000 there that day and, to the current day, every single Coventry fan remembers that day – it was one of the best in the club's 100-year history. Within a minute we were ahead, Nicky Platnauer diving to head in a ball almost at ground level. You thought then that you'd scored way too early and there was plenty of time for Liverpool to take stock and bounce back. But it didn't happen. Gibbo added two before half-time and we walked off to a standing ovation from a disbelieving crowd. Liverpool were that good and we were 3-0 up. They hadn't lost for two months and the following weekend would beat Notts County 5-0.

In the dressing room Bobby, along with us, was stunned at what he'd just witnessed. He challenged us to repeat the first half, but we all thought they'd sort themselves out, reorganise and beat us because that's what they did every week and had done for many years. John Motson paid tribute to me in the second half with 'if only every team would use a winger and get the ball wide the way Dave

Bennett has gone wide for Coventry today, football would be a lot better to watch'.

The clock ticked on, the floodlights kicked in on a cold afternoon and with six minutes remaining Gibbo completed his hat-trick with a brilliant curler past Bruce Grobbelaar. John Motson summed it up: 'What a marvellous day for Terry Gibson and for the supporters, six minutes from the end and they've made it four, their form this season is no fluke.' The feeling after that game was that we'd given Liverpool their biggest defeat in years. We had … Coventry City! We were wondering what we could do next and where we could go from there. Everybody started looking at us, everybody was watching us and analysing us. We were happy but we hadn't done anything yet. We'd won one game. You enjoy that moment but we hadn't really done anything at that point. We couldn't start singing and jumping around even though we'd had a great win. We wanted to kick on and carry on near the top of the table but we weren't quite there at that point. We weren't automatically thinking we were going to kick on from there even though we all wanted to do well.

Boxing Day was always a fixture to look forward to, the crowd swelled by fans back home for Christmas visiting family, almost a tradition of sorts. When you've got Manchester United as the visitors it's close to a sell-out, and a point took us unbeaten in nine. Then came home games against Sunderland and Watford as we moved into 1984. In conditions that were some of the worst I've ever played in, Highfield Road was like a lake as we beat Sunderland. To this day I don't know how the ball rolled on that pitch. After two replays against struggling Wolves to reach the FA Cup fourth round we witnessed one of the most freakish goals I've ever seen in a game I've been playing in. Watford's Steve Sherwood kicked deep into our half, the ball bounced once and sailed over Raddy into the net. No one knew what to do; you've the bizarre scene of the goalkeeper being congratulated by his team-mates. Raddy pleaded for a foul after he'd missed the ball, but referee Lester Shapter pointed to the centre spot. To round off a dismal day, Watford won it in injury time.

There began a run of 13 games without a win. If it could go against us, it did. Jason Dozzell became the youngest-ever First Division scorer against us for Ipswich, then Sheffield Wednesday, leading the Second Division, scored two late goals at Hillsborough to knock us out the FA Cup, and Raddy was sacked after errors in our defeat at home to Stoke, so Perry was back in goal. Arsenal beat us 4-1 at Highfield Road while down to ten men and with Pat Jennings off the pitch injured. Similar happened in the 3-3 with Villa when Peter Withe took over from the injured Nigel Spink.

Several of the players had moved from clubs where they weren't regulars, so playing week in, week out at the highest level was something we hadn't factored in; fatigue was playing a part and we just couldn't stop the rot. Bobby was always trying to fix it. We were training every day. Sometimes you'd be thinking maybe we should have a day off here or there but Bobby was working hard and so were the rest of us. Some of the players were tired because we were doing a lot of fitness work. Bobby was a fit bloke and he'd lead a lot of that and do the running with us. We had to up our fitness because he thought we might not have been fit enough. He was trying to fix it all, plug gaps where there weren't any gaps, and sometimes he wasn't looking in the right places. It just wasn't gelling. Bobby was trying to put these teams together but it wasn't quite working. Maybe some of the older players didn't want to play for him. We lost one, then two and then all of a sudden it was eight, nine and more, and we were wondering where we were going. Bobby was very up and down, along with the results. He was very passionate and really cared about the job. We all cared. Yes, it's the manager who gets the boot if things aren't going well, but this was my job as well and the players had to do what we could to stop the rot.

Then Bobby played a trump card, bringing in Birmingham's Mick Ferguson on loan until the end of the season. Mick had left Coventry in the summer of 1981 after a very successful time alongside Ian Wallace. It was unusual to loan a player from one of your rivals, especially with us in 16th place. By now Dave Bamber had played his last game for the club and joined Walsall, while Harry Roberts and Steve Hunt also departed, for Birmingham and West Brom. Tommy Langley, the former Chelsea striker, played a couple of times, and that was all it took for Bobby to bring in Mick, who gave us a partnership with Gibbo and some much-needed experience.

Mick also gave us goals as we took three points against both Wolves and Forest. Back-to-back wins gave us some much-needed breathing space and restored belief and confidence. It was a real battle around us with five matches to play, which included trips to Southampton, Manchester United and Liverpool. Luton, and Norwich on the final day, were our chances to get valuable points at Highfield Road. That season Southampton finished runners-up to Liverpool; they had an outstanding season and played fantastic football. We'd concede 17 goals in those three away games. United won 4-1, then it all fell apart at The Dell. Lloyd McGrath made his debut at centre-half alongside Steve Jacobs, and we were thrashed 8-2. Both Danny Wallace and Steve Moran scored hat-tricks as we slipped back to 17th.

With my little brother Gary and my parents.

Boys in Blue – the 1978/79 Manchester City squad line up.

Spot the ball! Chasing possession for Manchester City against Crystal Palace, November 1979.

Jostling for position in a 1979 Manchester derby with United's Kevin Moran.

Keeping a close eye on my brother, Gary, while we both play for Cardiff against Charlton, December 1981.

Causing problems for the Peterborough defence in the FA Cup fifth round, 1981.

My first taste of Wembley – the 1981 FA Cup Final.

Going in hard but fair in the challenge against Steve Perryman in the 1981 FA Cup Final.

Grabbing a goal in a 2-1 Milk Cup win for Cardiff over Hereford, August 1982.

Racing for the ball against QPR, now for Coventry.

Keeping my eye on the ball for Coventry, 1985.

Can't beat a kickabout in the street!

Waiting for the FA Cup draw with the lads.

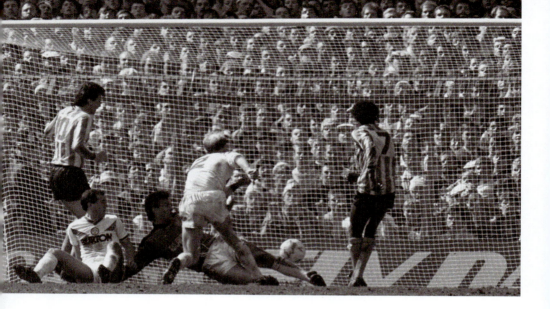

On our way to Wembley! I net the winner in extra time of our FA Cup semi against Leeds United.

Those celebrations after the Leeds FA Cup win just kept on going!

Gibbo hadn't scored since the draw with Villa in March but returned to form with a late equaliser in the next game against Luton. We held on for 43 minutes at Anfield but by 82 minutes it was 5-0 and Ian Rush had four to his name. Big Sam was now back in the defence and with just Norwich to play we started the day level on points with both Stoke and Birmingham. We'd conceded almost two goals a game, the defence was shell-shocked and Perry in goal was still only 17. We were happy to be playing at home knowing that we had to win, as we backed ourselves at home. Norwich weren't the toughest side to play so we fancied our chances. We knew we just had to win.

Bobby spoke to us prior to kick-off and asked where we wanted to be playing next season. As it stood, if we were relegated we'd face the likes of Oxford and Wimbledon, who were starting to move through the divisions. He then left us alone and went back to his office. Talk about pressure when John Deehan put Norwich ahead. Fortunately for us, Mick Ferguson levelled immediately but at this point we were down. Just 12 months earlier I was sealing promotion for Cardiff, but out on the pitch that day at Highfield Road you could hear transistor radios around the ground as fans listened in to what was happening with the teams around us. You could sense the anxiety as the crowd was willing us to score, and with 20 minutes left we were awarded a corner out on the right side. You practise for these moments, and you're entrusted with delivering the right ball at the right time into the right areas. I was surprised it went past Chris Woods as he fumbled it into the net at the near post.

I had a bit of a habit of getting goals in big games. People after that said I was a player for the big games and that I came alive when it mattered. Now, maybe part of it was that I'd come from Manchester City and I'd already played in big games, I'd already played in front of big crowds, I'd already played in a cup final. Compared to some of the players at Coventry at that time I'd played in more big occasions, I'd witnessed the big atmospheres and maybe that helped me do well in big games. Put it this way, I always turned up on the big days. Having said that, I've always said it wasn't that I came alive in the big games, it was that I got more of the ball in them. If it was a big game or a game against one of the top sides, then my team-mates would get the ball to me. If we were playing against a lower side and were 1-0 up early on, then I'd hardly get a kick because they didn't need to get the ball out to me. Instead, I'd keep my shape and focus more on helping out the fullback and do my job.

Sometimes it was more about stopping the opposition playing and making sure they didn't cause us any problems. The crowd might not be happy with those kinds of games because they want to see the highlights of me beating a man or scoring a goal, but my team-mates would appreciate it.

In those big games, the team would rely on me to do something, a little bit of magic, like I did against Norwich. The importance of the game made it such a vital goal, although we did still have plenty of time left for Norwich, who were safe, to bounce back. Which they so nearly did. There were 86 minutes on the clock when a cross came in from their right and Robert Rosario, who wasn't renowned as a prolific scorer, headed it back across Perry Suckling, where it bounced against the post, across the goal and into his arms. The collective sigh of relief could be heard around the stadium. We knew at that point that we were going to stay up, that little bit of luck was with us. We'd made it difficult in the previous weeks but we got ourselves over the line, thankfully. When the final whistle blew you had the iconic picture of Bobby clenching his fists on the pitch with chairman Iain Jamieson next to him. We'd been favourites for the drop but had stayed up, just, as Birmingham drew with Southampton and joined Notts County and Wolves in the Second Division. The irony, of course, is that Mick Ferguson's three goals in seven games relegated his parent club and manager Ron Saunders. Mick did the job he was brought in for, alongside Gibbo, who scored 17 league goals in 35 games, some effort in his first full season in the top flight. Mick returned to Birmingham after being unable to agree a contract with Bobby, then signed for Brighton.

We'd done it. We were happy. To score the winning goal that helped us stay up, I was more than happy. But I was already thinking about what was going to happen next season, what was the manager going to do? I enjoyed the moment, I was happy because I'd already been relegated in my career with Cardiff and it wasn't nice. I'd played for Man City when we got beaten by Halifax. I'd lost a cup final. I'd seen the ups and downs and emotion in football, and staying up on the final day was another to add to that. I'd experienced a lot as a young lad so scoring the winner on the last day, in a way it just felt like another game to me. A final-day winner to stay in the division? That was just another string to my bow.

We wanted to use it as a stepping stone and push on next season. I was just then thinking whether I'd still be involved in the team the next season. You know in football how things can change. When you're scrapping at the bottom of the table the manager could lose his job and when that happens you don't know if you'll be in the new manager's plans. It's like someone buying a new house but not liking the décor, so they rip it all out. It's like that with players, the new guy might come in and not like certain players and will change it. I was just hoping I'd be part of the décor at Coventry City for a long time and I wasn't going to be one of the pictures that got tossed in the bin.

5

History Repeating

I'D SCORED six times in 32 starts in the 1983/84 season, while Nicky Platnauer also scored six and was named player of the year, some achievement in his debut season in the First Division. We needed reinforcements during the summer and six new players joined, a mixture of hungry, lower league players and vast experience of the top tier. We also had a new chairman, as John Poynton took over from Iain Jamieson. Poynton had money to invest in the club and was born in the city.

We had this turnover of goalkeepers that Bobby needed to sort out that pre-season. Raddy had fallen out with the manager during the previous season after a bad performance, so Perry Suckling had come in. Raddy had a bad game and Bobby criticised him publicly afterwards. You think about things like that in that you have some managers who will have a go at you in public and you have some who will have a go at you in private. Bobby had a go at him in the changing rooms and we thought maybe he went a little bit over the top, and then Raddy shouldn't have reacted the way he did. It was probably down to the manager to then have a word with him the next day. In those days, if you fell out with the manager you wouldn't train with the first team, you were left out. That's where there can be a lack of respect, and instead of bringing someone back in they're cast out.

Someone like Ron Atkinson, who I played under at Sheffield Wednesday, would back players publicly and then hammer you behind closed doors. If you made a mistake under Big Ron he'd let you know in the changing rooms. He was one of those managers who if a player had a go at another player, he'd encourage that. Some managers say they have a go at the players and that's it, but Ron was one who'd encourage the flare-ups between players. I didn't like that because sometimes those flare-ups could escalate. They could come on to the training pitch and go further and further, and then people aren't getting on. I don't think that's the right way.

Anyway, Bobby criticised Raddy and we went through these goalkeepers until Steve Ogrizovic came in from Shrewsbury after two consistent seasons there. Oggy came in and never missed a game. We had Jake Findlay and then Oggy came in, and I don't think Jake has played a game since! Oggy had been number two to Ray Clemence during Liverpool's glory years but needed game time and he was a big presence for us. A further big presence was Notts County's Brian 'Killer' Kilcline. Not many players got past him or beat him in the air, and he didn't miss many games. We expected big things of his partnership with Trevor Peake and needed stability in the centre of our defence, as there had been too many changes the previous season, and we needed to build combinations around the pitch.

With Stuart Pearce established at left-back, Kirk Stephens joined us from Luton. Kirk was from Nuneaton and had played for the Borough before his move to Kenilworth Road. Ashley Grimes joined Luton as part of the deal; it hadn't really worked out for him at Coventry, but it would under David Pleat's management. Bob Latchford had broken the transfer record when he signed for Everton and he became their leading goalscorer post-war. He was 33 when we signed him, along with Wolves' Kenny Hibbitt and West Brom's Martin Jol. With Gerry Daly, Steve Jacobs and Big Sam Allardyce moving on, there was little remaining of the Gordon Milne/Dave Sexton era at the club.

Bobby brought in some impressive players but we must have had a turnover of 15 or 16 players, maybe even more. A lot of them, like Raddy and Dave Bamber, came in one season and then the following season a lot of players left. His success rate probably outweighed the ones he had to get rid of, though. You had this group of players that he brought in who stayed for longer than a year and bedded into the team. I'm talking about the likes of myself, Trevor Peake, Brian Kilcline, Micky Gynn, Oggy – these players went on to have success, so you've got to say that Bobby did well. Saying that, there were some of Bobby's signings that came in and didn't quite hit it off. Some of them didn't quite cut it and had to be moved on. It's difficult when you've got that turnover of players. We could never settle as a team because we were always playing with different players. You'd train with them and then all of a sudden the next player was coming in. I might be putting crosses in when the striker liked more of a cut back, and then you do that, but now it's a different striker who wants the ball on his head. As much as you work on things in training, you've got to actually get to know players to really play with them to the best of your abilities.

Of those players that Bobby brought in there was a nucleus of five or so who formed the backbone of the success that was to come. But that was the five or so who stuck around so we were able to get to know each other and find out what made each other tick on and off the park. That was a big part of our success to come, but unfortunately it didn't work straight away under Bobby. With all those players coming in we had all of these characters and the key was gelling those characters together. Eventually we did that but it happened after Bobby had left, as we'll come on to later. He brought all these players to the club but he was sacked before we all really gelled together and found success.

***

Pre-season had taken us to Sweden for 11 days, where we also lost to the Finnish national side, before six days in Scotland, stopping via Carlisle for a game, before Newport concluded the flurry of fixtures. George Dalton's introduction of his cricket bat saw Oggy's eyes light up. Most people wanted to be on his side; when you hear he bowled Viv Richards off a no-ball in the NatWest Trophy for Shropshire against Somerset, why wouldn't you? When Micky Gynn caught him out, he proceeded to chase him round the pitch. With Gynny's pace, Oggy had no chance. This gave us the opportunity to knit together as a team and we really needed experience to give us that extra know-how, which we could have done with at the end of the previous season. Trevor Peake was our new captain; he'd done the job at Lincoln for a few years and was a wise appointment to take us forward.

As with the previous season, we were among the favourites for relegation. The first eight games brought one win, home to Leicester, and we nose-dived out of the Milk

Cup after an embarrassing 3-0 home defeat to Walsall. Our win against Leicester was marred by crowd trouble from the very first minute. There were pockets of fighting breaking out all over the ground, first in the West Stand, then in the Main and then it all spilled on to the pitch. We were taken off for ten minutes while Bobby addressed the fighting factions with the Tannoy microphone to appeal for calm; we'd never seen anything like it. There's a picture in the *Got, Not Got* book of Oggy and Stuart Pearce watching while the chaos ensued around them.

Bobby brought in Don Mackay as his assistant, a further experienced head, but it just wasn't going for us. We had Killer's red card before half-time against Manchester United, and Arsenal scoring two in the last five minutes after Kenny Hibbitt's penalty was saved by Pat Jennings. Bob Latchford had started well but injuries put paid to him through the autumn spell, and the board, backed by John Poynton's investment, brought in two marquee signings in Cyrille Regis and Peter Barnes. Cyrille signed for £300,000 from West Brom, a surprise move at the time as a year previously players were leaving the club after being declined a £50-a-week rise, and we were all told similar in contract talks. Suddenly Cyrille's in the building and then Peter arrived, and he certainly wasn't on £300 a week, which we were then. There was immediate pressure on them to perform. Cyrille would be judged on goals and Peter on his supply line for the strikers.

Transfer fees were now over the £1m mark. Back in the summer Ray Wilkins moved from Manchester United to AC Milan for £1.5m, Paul Walsh moved from Luton to Liverpool for £700,000, while Graeme Souness left for Sampdoria with £650,000 changing hands. Mark Hateley to AC Milan from Portsmouth was just under the million-pound fee also. Cyrille was 26 when he signed for us, in the prime of his career after seven years at The Hawthorns.

Signing Cyrille was fantastic for me. With Cyrille, and then Lloyd McGrath, I had other black players in the team and we could make a stand about racism that we encountered on the pitch from the opposition. You had to make a stand, take things in your own hands and let them know you're not going to be a pushover. If the fans see it, the manager sees it, the opposition sees that you're scared, then they've won the battle. Racism does come into that because they'd call me names to put me off. Some were more serious than others. Some meant it, some would apologise afterwards, some wouldn't. You had all of that building like dynamite, ready to explode.

In fact, that was ready to explode before I even went on to the pitch because I knew some players would kick me, some would say this and that, and it was all to put me off my game. If someone made a racist remark, his team-mates might come over and say, 'Oh, he didn't mean that.' A lot of the time I'd confront people in the tunnel. You had to confront it. If I didn't say anything, he'd do it again and then his mate would do it. Sometimes I was the only black guy in the team and that was difficult. Some team-mates would back me if someone made a racist comment to me on the pitch. Some players would back you, some might just tell you to leave it. When Cyrille and Lloyd joined, we'd talk about these players. We'd talk to each other about who said what and it helped us develop an understanding of different players and how to react to it. It wasn't nice.

Sometimes you'd tell a referee or a linesman about a racist comment and they'd just tell you to get on with it. When we witnessed racism on the pitch or when we went out, we had each other to talk to. There weren't many up-and-coming black players playing in the First Division at that time so we could bounce off each other. We'd go to certain grounds and have racist remarks shouted at us and I'd want to do something about it, and Cyrille would calm me down. Then something else would happen and he'd want to do something about it, and I'd calm him down. We had a great relationship on and off the park. We were standing up to racism together and that helped our bond get stronger and stronger as friends, team-mates and as trailblazers for young black players coming into the game.

All of what we experienced just showed me what I was up against right from the early days. It made me realise what I was going to get. I had to show a little bit of cockiness and show that I didn't care, when actually I did care. I learned a lot about myself in those days from how I reacted to things and how I dealt with things. I had to battle it. I couldn't run away from it, I could never hide. Running away from it would show me to be a defeatist. I couldn't do that. I'd have been proving them right, like when they said things such as how the black guys loved it when it was nice and sunny but couldn't play in the cold, or didn't fancy it. I had to show them that we weren't like that.

As the years went on I learned what to say to these people. One of the best things I learned came from Jim Davidson. Around this time, he had this character called Chalky White that was his alter ego. When someone said something racist to me I'd talk like Chalky and say something like, 'Don't worry about it, Chalky is round your house banging your missus right now.' That won the fight for me without having to say anything else. I didn't have to fight them, they ended up wanting to fight me. Thanks for that, Jim!

Steve Ogrizovic says on the subject:

> Dave was always a big voice in the changing
> room. He needed to be as a black player playing

back then because those guys were guiding lights for what was to come. We had Dave, Lloyd and Cyrille, and they were very close in the changing room. As players in those days we probably didn't understand the difficulties that black players had; maybe we should have understood more. I think there's much more of an understanding nowadays. It must have been tough for those players to operate, especially when you went away from home. That took some guts. You had to be tough to do that and Dave was certainly tough.

Lloyd McGrath adds:

Big Cyrille took the brunt of the racism, to be honest. Cyrille and Dave looked after me more than anything else. It was nice to have two other black players in the team with you to help because of the racism that you would get. They helped me find a way to handle it and we had each other to speak to if we came up against it. That dressing room was crazy. We had big Cyrille, who was a big name but he was a down-to-earth character. You had Benno, who was larger than life but he was down to earth as well. Nobody in that dressing room thought they were better than anyone else. The bond that we had on and off the pitch was fantastic. I've never seen that anywhere else.

Having played against Micky Gynn for Manchester City in his Peterborough days I knew a bit about him, but what surprised me was his love of soul music and jazz. He was the last person I expected to have a love for it, and he knew his stuff. We used to go to concerts with Cyrille, and on the day of games we'd get focused and put a bit of Maxi Priest or Aswad on the stereo. We knew some of these artists and used to meet them at concerts. There was a lot of brilliant music around then. Cyrille and I went to see Maxi at the Mercia Sporting Club on Lockhurst Lane. He lived in Wolverhampton, Maxi, and we'd get the VIP treatment and not have to queue up. Maxi was a massive artist in the mid-1980s and we used to play his music on the coach during the FA Cup run.

* * *

Cyrille's debut against Newcastle saw Kenny Hibbitt fire home a fabulous free kick to save a point but we hovered around the relegation zone and took some heavy defeats, at Chelsea (6-2 after leading 2-0), West Brom (5-2, Cyrille's first goal for us) and a 5-1 thumping at Leicester. We were struggling for goals, even with a front four of Cyrille, Gibbo, Peter Barnes and myself. A Boxing Day defeat at Luton saw Bobby sacked with us one place off the bottom of the table. We'd won fewer than ten games all year and John Poynton stepped in. He wanted change and wanted improvement, so Don Mackay took over – I was hoping he liked the décor and wanted to keep me around.

Things hadn't been going well for a while under Bobby. Towards the end of 1984, results weren't great. We lost one game and then, before you know it, you're losing three, four, five, six on the trot. That happens in football, it's easy to get into a slump like that and can be very difficult to get out of it, and we found it difficult to get out of that slump. You learn about the players at times like that. We were learning about each other because we were a new team and we had this turnover of players. Someone like Trevor Peake was a great defender but in those early days he was playing with different centre-halves and you didn't see how good he was until the next year or the year after when some of the newer players went and the ones that were left gelled and formed the nucleus of a really good side. We had to get to know each other as players and as people. Once you get to know your team-mates personally you can trust them. With Trevor Peake, for example, as we played together and got to know each other, you find out his strengths as a player, but also things like what you can say to him and what you can't say to him, how he'd take it. That kind of thing helps. We all grew as a team and as friends.

When things aren't going well, sometimes players lose respect for the manager. It all depends how the manager treats you. On a personal level the manager might be alright with you but the team just isn't playing well. Bobby was always good with me. I remember Malcolm Allison going at Manchester City and he gathered all of us at the training ground and thanked every one of us. Bobby was just gone. One day he was there, the next he wasn't. Bobby had signed me so of course I was disappointed to see him leave. The way the team was going, though, you had to wonder if it was what was best for the team. But Bobby had signed me and we'd never fallen out or had any bad words to say to each other. Maybe it was the right time for him, though. Who knew why it wasn't working for Bobby? Perhaps it could have been losing the changing room or certain players not playing for him but, nonetheless, I was sad to see him go. I don't have any bad words to say about Bobby Gould.

Don took charge and obviously, having already been at the club, he knew the players and, as an assistant, you're just a different voice who might do things a little bit differently to the manager, but the manager would have the last word. This was Don's chance to step up and have that responsibility. He already knew the set-up. You bring a brand-new manager in and they want to bring in their own people, change things, and it might take some time to gel. Don had been a goalkeeper, and his assistant was Frank Upton. Frank had different ways of coaching that some of us didn't agree with. We didn't enjoy his training or a lot of the work that he wanted to do with us in the gym. Some of us told him we weren't happy with his way of working but he just carried on as he was. We had meetings as players and put our point across, and the senior pros would try to speak to Frank and Don.

Promoting Don gave him the chance to hit the ground running and, to begin with, he did. We thumped Stoke on New Year's Day and Gibbo gave us victory at Old Trafford in the game that saw Bryan Robson collide with the advertising hoarding and dislocate, for the first time, his shoulder. Gibbo partnered Cyrille and remembers well their partnership:

> People say it didn't work out for Cyrille initially at Coventry, but it was me scoring the goals, Benno crossing the ball and Cyrille would get the flick-ons and occupy defenders so I could

capitalise. He held the ball up so well. I saw a player that was irritated by the fact he was being judged purely on scoring goals. If you combined his goals with mine, we'd be over 30, which was a decent return in the First Division. Great guy and a real privilege to play in the same team.

It was a good start but then we went and lost the next three on the trot. Don brought in a couple of players who could play on the right, one of whom was Andy Williams, and all of a sudden I was thinking my position was under threat. I was thinking Don must have thought these players were better than I was and could offer something I couldn't, so I wasn't happy. I had to fight for my place and show that I was better than these new players coming in. If a manager buys new players, though, then they have to play them and show some faith in them. From then on the relationship between myself and Don was frosty. I managed to keep my place a lot of the time but I knew if I got injured he had someone ready to take my place and I might struggle to then get back in. I had to be at my best all the time.

We splashed out a lot of money on a guy from Hearts called Dave Bowman, who came in to play in the middle of the park. It didn't work out for him, though. It wasn't long before results weren't going that well for Don. On the pitch we were playing a similar way to how we had under Bobby. Don took over from Bobby with 21 league games still to play that season. After 18 of them, we'd won seven, which wasn't too bad, but we'd lost ten, drawing only one. That run had put us bang in trouble at the wrong end of the table. It meant that we went into the final three games of the season needing to win all three to survive. To win three in a row was massive, as we hadn't won three league games on the trot all season. We'd only won two on the trot twice, so to have to win three was a huge ask. When you think of it now it was mind-boggling.

Something else that now appears mind-boggling is that after a flu epidemic saw the cancellation of our early April fixtures, we'd fallen behind the other teams with the season due to end on 11 May. The FA rearranged the three fixtures, against Stoke, Luton and Everton, for the end of the season, with two after the FA Cup Final, which was always the last game. We also had Ipswich at Portman Road to add to these games after another postponement. After Sunderland won at Highfield Road after Easter, we were 18th. This was the first season I'd played against my brother in a proper professional game. We'd drawn at Roker Park in September but there was more riding on the return at the business end of the season. Our parents were in the crowd, and this was the game when Gibbo's penalty was saved by

Chris Turner. To this day I still can't work out how my shot in the last minute didn't go in. It hit Gary and went straight up and over the bar. You could see the disbelief in the eyes of the fans on the West Terrace. Nine times out of ten they hit the roof of the net, and we should have scored in the second half, but Turner was outstanding. I remember Gary looking over at me after he'd blocked my shot. I couldn't believe it hadn't gone in. From our parents' perspective a draw would have been a fair result, but it amplified the pressure on us with ten games to play.

The size of the task was emphasised after a mixed spell of results. Killer hit the bar at Ipswich on a wet and cold night in East Anglia, but we walked off the pitch knowing we had to beat Stoke, Luton and Everton to stay up, nothing else would suffice. By this point everyone had finished their fixtures. Sunderland and Stoke had been relegated, which was bad news for Gary, of course. Stoke had an awful season. They had players of the calibre of Steve Bould, Paul Dyson, Mickey Thomas, George Berry, Sammy McIlroy, Keith Bertschin and Mark Chamberlain, yet they won three games all season and lost 31. They only scored six goals away from home and ended up 33 points from safety, a staggering decline with the players they had. Luton were mid-table and Everton were league champions, by 13 points, and would win the European Cup Winners'

Cup in Rotterdam 11 days before our game. Bear in mind also that they faced Manchester United in the FA Cup Final eight days before our game, it was crazy. We'd play them on 26 May when most teams would be on the beach.

Talk about drama. We headed for the Potteries to face Stoke, and even given their position it was never an easy place to visit. No one prior to these games had raised any doubts or concerns about why we were allowed to play our three games after everyone else. I think they just assumed we wouldn't win them and that it was a foregone conclusion. Football was just waiting for our inevitable relegation to the Second Division. Norwich were the only team we could catch with this eight-point gap, and remember we'd only won back-to-back games twice all season. If we'd have won three on the bounce earlier, we wouldn't have been in this position.

The Victoria Ground, Stoke, could hold 35,000 during the 80s but on this occasion it was just under 7,000, with a few thousand Coventry fans making the journey. It was Stoke's last game before relegation, but give it a few years and we'd come across the famous old ground once more. Talk about tense. Stuart Pearce smashed home a penalty just after the hour and the clock ticked down until, with five minutes remaining, Cyrille clashed with Paul Dyson and referee Neil Midgley blew for a second penalty, for

Stoke. We couldn't believe it. You could hear the fans reduced to silence, they were as stunned as we were, that sinking feeling. Ian Painter put the ball on the spot; it was unbelievable. All eyes were on Oggy. Painter was their top scorer with six goals and four of those were penalties. The omens weren't good.

We're all on the edge of the penalty area poised to close in on any rebounds, more in hope than expectation, but its good habits you're taught from an early age to expect the unexpected from 12 yards. Lots was going through my mind. I was thinking if it went in then we were down. I got set and waited. And then it happened. Ian Painter smashed the ball against the underside of the bar. There was no contentious 'did it cross the line' questions, we cleared the rebound and breathed a huge sigh of relief. He'd hit it that hard that it hit the bar and rebounded back outside the 18-yard box. Play to the whistle. We'd got away with it but the game wasn't over. We still had to get back, chase back, stop the crosses, all of that.

My emotions were down when he stepped up for the penalty and then sky high when he missed it, but we all had to do our jobs because there were still a few minutes to play. We couldn't go and throw it away from there, not after what had just happened. We just couldn't throw it away. They'd given us a chance by missing the penalty, so we couldn't let them back in. The wait for the final whistle seemed like an eternity and then suddenly questions started to be asked, discontent in the football world as we could just win these three games. We had six days to wait for the visit of David Pleat's Luton. In their goal was Les Sealey, who'd left us in the summer of 1983 under a cloud and would have a point to prove on one of the biggest nights in the club's history.

It's a cliché but we had to take it one game at a time. You couldn't think ahead and about what would happen if we went down, as on a personal level some players would have to leave the club if we were relegated. You couldn't think like that. You couldn't think of it as three games. It was one at a time, play each game as it is. Win one then think about the next one. Our careers were on the line, but our careers were on the line depending on how we performed against Stoke first of all, then Luton and then finally Everton. You might think that the Everton game would the hardest because they were the champions, and you might have thought Luton or Stoke would be easier. They were never going to be any easier. If we didn't perform against Stoke then that was it. Play badly against Stoke and you knew you wouldn't be in the team for the next two games and then you wouldn't be at the club the next year regardless of what happened. The manager was trusting the players he picked to go out and win these games. That was a massive amount of trust because it meant you had the club, the fans and your team-mates in your hands, as well as your own livelihood. No pressure! If you're part of the Coventry team that gets relegated from the top flight, those fans will remember that and associate you with that for the rest of their lives.

We wanted to win these games for ourselves. We wanted to do it for the manager as well. We desperately wanted to stay in the top division. Luton was a tough game. Oggy made a good save in the first half, I had a shot cleared off the line in the second half, and we had a stonewall penalty turned down. As the game was going on it was still 0-0. Then Killer popped up with a goal to give us the win that we needed. It was a scrappy game but we managed to get the 1-0 win that meant we went into the final game still in with a chance. But the game was against the champions, Everton. They'd already won the league so there wasn't anything riding on the game for them. It was a huge turnaround because the year before we played them at the end of the season and they had to get a result to stay up. This year we needed the result and they were the champions.

We knew that if we beat Luton, then Everton had a European game coming up and there were international matches approaching. We knew they wouldn't want to get hurt. We got among them and got into the tackles. They had other things on their minds. Football is a lot about psychology, and when you've got Everton with that mindset and then Coventry who were fighting for their lives down at the bottom, it makes a difference. We were going to kick, scrap and give them everything, we were going to let them know that we were there. They didn't want to do any of that and we knew it. We had to just get in among the tackles. We knew if they played a full-strength team we could close them down rapidly and get among them. The psychology was that we were in a battle and they weren't going to win the battle. We had to show Everton that we meant business.

We got right at them and took the lead through a Micky Adams goal. Cyrille had a fantastic game and got our second goal. We were cruising but then Paul Wilkinson scored for Everton to make it 2-1 before half-time, which created a few nerves. He was a livewire for them because he'd come in for Andy Gray and was trying to stake a claim for a regular place in the team. We went in at half-time at 2-1 and we just recircled, we regrouped and chatted about what we were going to do. We knew we had to get back among them. Cyrille scored again after half-time to make it 3-1 and by then it was all over. By then it was all about how many we were going to score. Southall kept the score down after that before Gibbo got the fourth for it to finish

4-1. We battered them in the end and Neville Southall did well to keep the score down. Cyrille did well in that game. He hadn't set the season alight with goals but we needed him and Gibbo up there bouncing off each other.

Because of this situation, they now make sure everyone kicks off on the final day at the same time because people said that we gained an advantage because we knew what we had to do. The thing was, we still had to go and win all three games. That wasn't necessarily an advantage because we had to win all three anyway to stay up. We just went into the game keen to do what we had to do and then everything would take its course.

It was a similar feeling to the year before. I thought, *We've done it again. I can't be doing this again though!* We were getting a reputation for winning our last game and these great escapes. It was a tremendous feeling to stay up like that but we wanted to push on into pre-season and improve. We didn't want to be fighting at the bottom again. We could look ahead to next season and look out for the fixtures with smiles on our faces. Everyone was happy. It was a happy squad.

Team spirit was really important to us staying up in the 84/85 season, and then to a lot of what we went on to achieve. It's a big part of the game. You might go out for a drink with a team-mate and find out they're having problems at home, and you might not have known that if you hadn't gone out with them. What that means is that when it comes to training, if you know someone is having problems, you might not have a go at them when they make a mistake. You can pull the lads in and let them know that this guy's having problems or his little one is having problems or his missus isn't well. You help each other. Also, if you have that positive relationship with your team-mates, then when you do tell them to get stuck in or whatever, it's taken in the right way, it's taken as encouragement and not that you're having a go at them.

At this point that team was still getting to know each other a little bit. You still had little cliques. But as we moved into the next season we had a backbone of the squad that had been together for the previous two seasons. We used to go out together and could talk and open up to each other. Things were looking up off the pitch but little did we know that on the pitch we'd be facing yet another scrap at the bottom.

6

The Hat-Trick of Great Escapes

WE WENT into 1985/86 thinking that we couldn't be scrapping at the bottom of the table again. We'd had some tough times in the previous two seasons with battling at the wrong end of the table. Attendances were down and we had some poor runs at home. With the crowd, I've always thought of them in thirds. One-third of the crowd loves a player who dribbles with the ball. One-third prefers a player who gets stuck in. One-third just likes a certain kind of player. So you might have two-thirds of the crowd against you because you're not the type of player they like to watch. That's before you even start. When you're on a bad run you can come out and the fans boo your name when it's read out. That's hard. You want the fans to encourage you and get behind you. That's why you see players run to certain bits of the ground when they score. They do that because season ticket holders sit in the same place every game, they don't move, so when you come out and hear them shouting, you get to know where they are.

You get stick as a footballer when you're not doing well, and then I might get down the wing, cross it on to someone's head and it's 1-0, and that same fan will say, 'Well, that's just what he's supposed to do,' and then his mate will say, 'He didn't do anything else all game.' You can't please everybody and not everybody was pleased at that time because of our home form. It's hard when you're losing. The fans want you to do well, but when you're not they can give you a hard time and we had that on occasions. It can be a daunting place to go out on to a football pitch. It might get to the point where you get so much abuse that some players don't want to go out there. We wanted to turn things around as we went into the new season and give the supporters plenty to cheer about.

We had some activity in the transfer market that summer. Ian Butterworth and Stuart Pearce both left to go to Forest. Pearce went on to become a legendary player but at the time he left Coventry he wasn't a big player, he was still finding his feet. We weren't losing a superstar. Greg Downs came in at left-back and Brian 'Bugsy' Borrows at right-back, both of whom became important players for us. They gelled into the team quickly, as Greg recalls:

I'd played against Dave a few times when I was at Norwich and he was at Man City. He wasn't a speedy winger who would just zip past you, he was more about guile and a really good touch. It's only when you play and train with somebody, though, that you really learn what they're like as a player. When I joined Coventry, I saw what Dave actually had. He was a great deliverer of the ball and he delivered it early when strikers wanted it putting in there. A lot of wingers will beat the full-back and then go back and beat him again. Dave had been coached well as a kid, and once George and John took over at Coventry that style of play really suited Dave.

He was a very effervescent character. He'd drive you nuts at times! We used to take the mickey out of him because he was always asking for lifts because he hadn't passed his test. I'd class Dave as a friend, not just a colleague. That was something that we had at Coventry. We were all mates in that team. That was special, you don't often get that. There's always someone who doesn't like someone else and that's natural, but that wasn't the case at Coventry. We all got on well together, we all accepted a bit of mickey taking and everything was in good taste, it was never nasty.

Brian and I built up a good understanding on the right-hand side. Quickly we knew each other's game, I knew what he was going to do and he knew what I was going to do. We knew where each other would be on the pitch at any time. Micky Adams was there as well, and we signed Nick Pickering around this time, so we had good competition at full-back. We were adding good players to the foundations we already had thanks to some of the players Bobby Gould had signed, like Killer, Oggy, Cyrille, Trevor Peake and myself. We'd had a massive turnover of players in those years so the management must have seen something in those players that were left. At this time you had to think about yourself because all these players were coming in and it was easy to wonder who'd come in next and whether they were coming in to replace you. It was healthy competition.

You wanted to be fit and firing in pre-season so you could get your name on the team sheet for the first match of the season. My thinking was that if I had the shirt then it was up to someone else to shift me. I just had to make sure I had that shirt for the first game of the season. Don had a pre-season with us for the first time and he got the miles in the tank with a fitness focus. He made sure that we were fit, we did plenty of running. I used to think, *When are we going to get a ball out?!* It felt like we'd never see a football again. It left us fit and ready for the season, though.

Despite some good players coming in and the good feeling around the club, we made a poor start. Don criticised the team in public and said it was a disgrace when we lost a 1-0 lead late on against Newcastle in the fourth game of the season, as we fell to a 2-1 defeat. I missed a chance in that one, trying to lob the goalkeeper. That defeat and a tendency of losing late goals was all part of us gaining experience. As you become more experienced you learn what to do, what to say and how to handle these situations. You learn how to see out a result in the closing stages. Don had a go at us after that game and maybe that was just inexperience from the players, some of us didn't know what to do in that situation.

As I went later into my career I realised that if you're not going to win a game then you need to make sure that you don't lose it. You learn to change your style of play to hold on to a lead. When you're inexperienced you sit back and drop deeper. As you learn, you might turn the opposition and have everyone push up, play that long ball and get everyone after it so it changes the game. We were learning the game all the time. We were still learning our trade at this point. We needed to have leaders on the pitch and we were getting there, we had seven, eight, nine players who were becoming captains. That's great because the manager can advise you, but once you cross the white line it's all about you as a player. In my Coventry career we had a group of players who you could say, 'Come on, you, get at it.' You could speak to each other on the pitch and say that we were changing it and we were going to knock it long, and everybody would be on the same page.

Unfortunately, we only won one of our first nine league games, a 5-2 victory over Oxford. That inconsistency from the previous season continued. We then beat West Brom and Leicester in back-to-back 3-0 wins and picked up some decent victories against the likes of Birmingham and QPR, but the winter saw us hit a wretched run. From 2 November to 18 January we played 14 games in all competitions, winning only two and losing ten of them. One potential issue from the season was that the captaincy changed. Trevor Peake was always the club captain but the team captain on the park moved from Trevor to Wayne Turner and then to Killer. Trevor was club captain and would handle the functions, sort the fines and that kind of thing. The team captain, that didn't really matter so much to be fair because on the pitch we had 11 captains. He'd just go toss the coin at the start, so it didn't make much difference.

In January 1986 we suffered a big loss – Terry Gibson was sold to Manchester United. We knew we were going to lose Gibbo because there had been interest from other sides and Coventry City has always been a selling club. You'd have players come and go and you had to adapt and push on. Gibbo was the latest big player to be sold. Don had a big job replacing him. We were struggling but still thought we had enough about us to stay in the division. Alan Brazil joined as part of the deal. He was only 26 but had suffered bad injuries already in his career. He came in as a big character. He loved his horse racing and I got on well with him. He did a job for us but only played 15 league games, scoring a couple of goals. Off the park he was a great lad. We wanted him to hit the ground running and be a goalscorer because, yet again, we were in a relegation battle. We had to just get through to the end of the season and then re-evaluate when we, hopefully, had stayed up. He was a great lad on a night out, though. I got on with him a little bit better than most.

Despite the best efforts of the players and staff we were still struggling on the pitch. As we came towards the end of the 1985/86 season we were in another relegation fight. We lost five in a row around the turn of the year in all competitions, and then between 8 March and 12 April we went eight without a win, losing six of them. The final straw was a 5-0 thrashing at the hands of Liverpool. It left us with three games to play, home to Luton, away to West Ham and then home to QPR on the final day. Don was sacked and we were left with three games to save ourselves. It was a difficult position to be in. West Brom and Birmingham were already dead and buried, so there was just one place left to play for. Oxford were in the last relegation place with 36 points from 38 matches. We were one point ahead but had played a game more, while there was a clutch of teams above us who could be dragged into it, including the likes of Aston Villa, Leicester and Ipswich.

It wasn't about the manager, it was about the players. We had to get it together, we had to put it right on the pitch. John Sillett and George Curtis took over as managers with just three games to save the club. It was a roll of the dice and the odds were perhaps against them. That's where the trust came in. We had to trust that what they were saying was right to keep us up and they had to trust us to do it on the pitch. It was John's first big job as a manager, it was a massive step up for him. He had to re-evaluate himself, the team and his staff. He'd have been wondering if he kept us up would he get the job full-time; if we went down would he still be given the job? It was a difficult situation for everyone. He'd already been at the club, he'd been Bobby's assistant but had left when they fell out, and he then came back under Don. He knew some of the players but had been working more with the youth team since coming back to the club. He was given an opportunity that he wanted to take with both hands.

He did something incredible right off the bat. A big changing point came when John Sillett came to us and asked us how we wanted to play. This was very different to what we'd been used to. We said we wanted to play to feet. He was worried that the big man, Cyrille, wasn't enjoying his football and he wanted to get the best out of him. We said we didn't want to play the long-ball game with Cyrille battling up in the air with his back to goal. We wanted to play in to his feet. John said fine. Then he did something even more incredible. He said if we won two out of the last three games of the season we'd all go to Spain. The lads went, 'What?! Spain?! Flippin' 'eck!' The lads were packing already! Win two out of three and we'd be off to Spain? We could do that. That brought everyone together. John wanted the team together, he was massive on camaraderie. He trained us hard, we worked hard but he wanted us to enjoy ourselves. John said he didn't want Cyrille running down the channels after the ball, he wanted him at centre-forward, with me getting crosses in for him. He said Cyrille wasn't someone who should be running into the channels all the time.

THE HAT-TRICK OF GREAT ESCAPES

We went into the first of these three massive games. We were up against Luton at home, another year with Luton playing a part in our survival. We won 1-0. We played well, should have had at least one penalty, had loads of chances and then Nick Pickering went and scored the winner for us. But then we lost away to West Ham, meaning we weren't safe on the final day and needed a win against QPR. Typical Coventry, we had to do it with the most tension possible instead of just beating West Ham and being safe!

On that final day it was a nervy experience despite the fact that we'd had two final-day escapes in the last two seasons. Sometimes John would tell you the team on a Friday before the game. You might go home and relax because you were playing, or sometimes you'd go away feeling nervous. Other times he might not have quite decided who he was going to play so he'd put 'From' and the squad that he was going to choose from, so you didn't know if you were playing until you got to the ground. With those final games it was nerve-wracking waiting to know if you were in the team or not. Everyone was nervous going into that last game. If you didn't have any nerves before a game like that then there's something wrong with you.

Two years earlier, Bobby had given us the team talk on the final day asking us who we wanted to be playing next season. This time it was John in the manager's seat and his focus was just on wanting us to play our game. We had no idea what was to come with John and what would happen the following season; we just had to win that game. It didn't matter what his tactics were that day – he could have played ten centre-forwards, we just had to get over the line.

Well, it was another big game and I popped up with the winner again! The big-game player! That really cemented that reputation for me – that I'd turn up in the big games. We didn't start well, though, as QPR took the lead. There we were, having had a bad season, 1-0 down in a game that we had to win. Killer equalised with a free kick. Typical Killer, it gently bobbled into the net … of course it didn't! Killer used to just smack it, he'd smash it. He had the most awkward strike of a ball I've ever seen. Usually with a free kick someone would roll the ball to the side to someone else to hit it. Killer wanted the ball rolled back towards him. He'd have to adjust his stride all the time because the ball was moving back towards him. It was the most unusual run-up he had for free kicks. It's a good job he could strike it so well. But if he was ten yards away I'd have to roll it quick enough to get to him but slow enough for him to adjust. If you rolled it too hard it would just hit him. He'd smash it, though. He was brilliant to play with because if we got a free kick early on, he'd come take it and we'd shout, 'Killer, smash it, hit his head off, smash it in his balls!' You'd see the players in the wall, they'd look at it and you could see they didn't fancy it. Killer would smash it and it might whack into the wall and fly off anywhere. That meant the next time we had a free kick you knew no one wanted to get into that wall. It worked every time, that came from experience. He's smashed the first one so on the next one the wall is terrified and doesn't want to get in the way of the ball. Because of that, he could smash it again or bend it, place it, it worked every time. It was the simplest free kick in the world but it worked.

Anyway, back to this particular free kick. At this point we're a goal down and staring at relegation. He was the nominated free kick taker, and we knew he'd smash it. The only problem was, if the keeper saved it or it hit the woodwork, the power Killer hit with meant you could forget about rebounds because it would bounce outside the box. He always fancied a free kick or penalty, though. We trusted him. We knew he wasn't going to place it, he went for raw power. He scored it and then my chance came. The ball came to me, I went around the goalkeeper and finished it with my left foot. Another big goal. Another big win. Another final-day escape.

We'd won two of the three games and John Sillett was good to his word and took us all to Spain. That's when we really got to know each other. That was huge. We spoke, we drank, we laughed, we got to know each other. It was a fantastic time and it showed on the pitch when we came back the following season. We were a different team. We'd experienced that winning feeling and some of what John wanted to do, and we wanted to taste more of it.

By the time we got to the end of that season we'd gelled as a team. As a group we were so close. That team that we had was put together with pretty much no money. It was a magnificent jigsaw that fitted together. He had the trust in us to go out together and we repaid that trust by not doing anything stupid. It makes a big difference when your manager trusts you like that. When you have that trust, you want to run for the manager, you want to play for him.

Me and Gynny loved our music. We were always gelling together even before that in the Don Mackay era because we'd go for a drink in the afternoon in the Blacksmiths up in Ryton. The lads used to read the riot act among ourselves. We were becoming a team off the park as well as on the park and people could dig each other out and it was taken the right way. We were becoming a unit. That unit just kept getting stronger and stronger.

We were a team. My thinking was that if the other players were playing well, my wife and kids live better. So we'd chat about things and sort problems out in the pub. You might not be getting on with your wife, you might have a sick child, your parents might be ill, all this kind of stuff you might not talk about unless you went out for a drink together. You've got people from different backgrounds, walks of life, religions, so the social side meant you got to know each other and, before you knew it, we were all friends. That all helps on the pitch. You'd get a lot of outsiders around you as well as a footballer, and if the whole team is together and on that level then you can look out for each other and avoid trouble. It's camaraderie. If you haven't got that, then you've got nothing. The successful teams all have that. You might not get players going out together now like we used to but you can still see the teams that have camaraderie when you see a goalkeeper running the length of the pitch to congratulate a goalscorer. That comes across in the way that a team plays. By 1986 we had that. When Greg Downs joined, he became our entertainment manager. When we got a fine, John and George would use the money to take the players' wives out.

Greg Downs reminisces on his role:

> My father had a pub, so when I was at Coventry I was the entertainment manager. The camaraderie at the club was great. I remember one time we had a reserve game and had organised a night out for the lads after it. We went down to Nobby's

bar, right in the city centre. We all went in there and all of a sudden in walked John and George. I've never seen so many lads run to the toilet so quickly! John and George walked in, said, 'Great, this is how it should be,' went straight to the bar and bought everybody a drink. They were very much into the team spirit. People didn't mind seeing us out when we were going well.

During the 1985/86 season we hadn't done well. We can all come up with excuses but really the style of play that the previous management wanted was not conducive to the group of players at all. For myself, I'd been at Norwich for ten years and always played good football. I came to Coventry and thought, *My god, what the hell has happened here?* I went to see the manager and asked why they had signed me because I'd never played that way in my life. Cyrille hated it as well because they wanted me to get the ball and whack it right up to Cyrille. That's no good, you don't play football that way. The atmosphere in the city completely turned around that year from 'bloody hell, they're not very good, are they?' to then that season under George and John it completely changed and we were passing the ball

THE HAT-TRICK OF GREAT ESCAPES

to feet. The supporters were enjoying the football and we were getting results.

Everything was positive when we went out. There was never any trouble. It was incredible that when we did go out there was never any trouble. We never had to look after each other. We were normal lads. There were no big-time Charlies in that squad. We went out and enjoyed ourselves and enjoyed each other's company. George and John were good man-managers. They knew the players liked to go and have a pint and they almost encouraged it. We had rules, though. You couldn't go out two days before a game, but even then I remember John turning to me and Cyrille one night and saying that we were 30-year-old men, if we fancied a pint on a Thursday night just go out to a country pub to have one.

For the Christmas party, we would organise a coach and all go in fancy dress to Kenilworth. We'd do a pub crawl down Kenilworth. I'd love to see some pictures of that. Can you imagine that today? Premier League footballers walking through Kenilworth on a pub crawl in fancy dress?! John's quote was to never go into the city until after 8pm because it wouldn't be a good look to be on the drink in the afternoon. Cyrille used to say something that Ron Atkinson had said to him, which was that we had to remember who we were, what we were and who we were representing.

The players would go out on a Wednesday, and you had to go out. You had to. No matter what. If you didn't go out you'd get a fine. If you were having problems at home you could come out for one drink and leave early, but you had to come out or you got fined. If we stayed out until one in the morning and you went home at nine at night, you'd just say the lads had stayed out to go for a curry. The wives would be out as well, you see, and they'd talk, so the lads would say it was just a curry when some of the lads were rolling in at one in the morning! But those nights out meant we all got to know each other and got to know about each other's families. Lads like me, Gynny, Cyrille and Lloydy loved our music and had a great time. We could only drink halves in those days. We couldn't drink pints, otherwise we'd get fined. As a group, we worked hard, we trained hard and we drank hard, even if it was just half a pint at a time! It was a unique relationship that we had as those lads. We laughed so much and we're still laughing today. With what was to come that following season, we'd certainly have plenty more to laugh about.

7
A New Era

WE FELT good going into the new season. We'd just avoided the drop, things were looking up and we were confident. We'd gone away to Spain, and John saw that as a bonding trip. He was very clever because he saw that as a reward for us staying up but it was also a chance for him to get to know the lads. It was a canny move. We enjoyed ourselves and were still finding things out about ourselves. It set us up for the new season. John and George were part of the group and would join in. They were getting to know our characters and learning what we were like, whether we were sociable, what we were like when we were socialising, did we mix and all of that. It was helping them to build up a portfolio of the players and their characters. It was showing them who they could rely on in the trenches.

It can be difficult for players in situations like that. Obviously, you're not going to be, let's say, very outgoing in front of your new manager. But John might come and buy the first round, get everyone to have a drink and relax and then he might go and do his own thing and leave the players for a while. You might then all meet up later on. It wasn't like John was with us all the time but we might end up in the same restaurant in the evening. He wasn't with us 24/7 but we were still sensible. No one broke his trust by being stupid and getting into bother. You have to have that trust and show that. He trusted us and he was getting to know us, so we all behaved.

John and George were different to Don and Bobby because they could be good cop, bad cop. George was more of the disciplinarian with things like you had to make sure you were clean-shaven. You had to wear a tie. You could only drink halves. You could never be late. If he said to be out for training at 10am then you had to be there. He kept on top of all of that. John was the one who'd put his arm around you and have a laugh with you. They worked it very well between them and that was exactly what we needed.

Another thing we needed was one or two fresh faces on the pitch and Dave Phillips and Keith Houchen came in that summer, as Keith explains:

> You always heard Benno before you saw him, he was a big character at the club. I had a lot of

football clubs in my time and it was very unusual to have a dressing room like the one we had at Coventry. We didn't just turn up for training and matchdays together, we did everything together as a squad. John and George were a big part of that and they made sure everyone was involved, including the wives and families. We all had a lot in common.

There was a lot of messing around in that dressing room, a lot of joking. None of it was nasty though. A lot of the time in football dressing rooms people try to do things that are funny but it isn't funny. At Coventry everything was open and above board, everybody was totally honest. It was the opposite side of that Crazy Gang Wimbledon kind of culture. They'd be winding people up in the tunnel before games with dances and ghetto blasters; we were completely different. We were all about the camaraderie.

We had a yellow jersey for the worst trainer each week. We voted each week for the worst trainer and they would have to wear this bright yellow jersey on a Friday. It was a secret vote. You'd get this little slip of paper and you'd write a name on it. It started off that you'd just write the person's name. These notes started getting more and more risky as everyone realised you could have a go at someone without anyone finding out who had written it. Benno came out of it with the name 'the cackling gambler', I'm not sure where that one came from!

These new faces were joining a settled team that had really gelled together by now. Guys like myself, Trevor Peake, Oggy, Killer, Micky Gynn; we'd been there for a few years and were really settled by now, meaning that we could help new players come in and settle. It was such a strong foundation to build from. This squad had battled against the odds together and had a real trust in each other. It helped as well that we were signing not just good players, but also good characters, the right characters. Keith came to us with the reputation for having scored big goals for Hartlepool, and Dave Phillips had a reputation for scoring great goals. They were good additions to the squad. We had players like Lloydy and Micky Gynn coming on well, the squad was getting stronger and we had a balanced side.

The players who signed, and the players who were already there, really suited the new way of playing with getting the ball on the ground and up to Cyrille. The whole team seemed stronger playing that way. It was a more technical way of playing and this group of players was up to that challenge. No disrespect to the players that had left in the years before but the group of players we had at the start of that season were up to getting to grips with that way of playing much quicker than the squads we'd had before. John and George would have seen in the final three games of the previous season and in training that we were suited and able to play in that style. I was happy to be playing to feet, happier than playing long-ball.

Pre-season itself under John and George was similar to what we'd done the previous years with Don and Bobby. They wanted us to work hard. They believed in putting the miles in. One difference was that they wanted us to get on the ball and work with the ball a bit more. Pre-seasons were always hard, though. I always used pre-season to get myself fit, whereas the players today come into pre-season already fit. I was lucky that I didn't put on or carry much weight and was quite nimble. Pre-season for me was all about getting back fit and getting ready for that first game of the season. I hated pre-season, though. It was always hard, my legs were always tired and I was always worried about getting injured before the big kick-off of the new season.

Once we got back from Spain we played a pre-season game against Chester and I said I wanted to play up front. Cyrille wasn't playing that day and I went up front and did really well. Then he tried me up there with Cyrille and we did really well together. It all kicked on from there. Dave Phillips or Micky Gynn would play wide right. John didn't want Cyrille down the flanks, he wanted him as the target man and I could run the channels. I always fancied myself as an inside-forward. We knitted together really well.

Keith Houchen:

> John and George weren't convinced that two big centre-forwards like me and Cyrille could play together and then I was injured at the start of the season so Benno played through the middle. He was one of those players who could play anywhere.

It helped that me and Cyrille were really good mates. We went out together, we drank together, so that partnership was just natural. That partnership was another piece of the jigsaw that came together that season. Playing with Cyrille was immense. He held the ball up so well. He was a big lad so not many people were going to knock him off the ball. That meant you could make runs off him because he could hold it up, lay it back and you could be running on. We got the best out of him. We knew he wasn't the best running down the channels. We knew if we got him into the box then he'd win the ball, he'd head it and bring players into play. He was so good in the 86/87 season especially. It was a pleasure to play with him.

He was also my best mate at the club at the time. We roomed together, we went out together, we played up front together, we did everything together. When he left the club he'd always ring me to tell me when he was coming back. You could see on the pitch how well we got on off it. As a man he was tremendous. I miss him every day. I've got a picture of him on a keyring that I keep with me so I've always got him with me. He's always with me in more ways than one. When we came together at Coventry it was like knife and fork coming together.

***

After all that we started with a 1-0 defeat to West Ham. But West Ham were a good side and a 1-0 defeat away from home wasn't a disaster. Let's not forget we'd only just stayed up on the last day the season before. We played okay and we were still getting used to this new way of playing. You can't judge anyone or anything on the first game, it was always going to take some time. The pundits would have been watching that first game and seeing us as relegation material and trying to write us off. We didn't see it like that at all and we were still upbeat. Upton Park was a difficult place to go, the crowd was right on top of you and for the first game of the season they were right up for it. Losing 1-0 wasn't that bad a result and it gave us an opportunity to be resolute.

Like I say, Upton Park was a hard place to go. Grounds like that and the Baseball Ground, the crowds were right on top of you. The Dell was another one; the pitch seemed so small and compact and the crowd were right there. You knew you were going to get a bad reception at these places. They were always hostile. You had to be mentally prepared for it because of how close the crowd were and at that time you got so much abuse chucked at you as the away side. You had to be mentally prepared. If you took a corner at Upton Park, The Dell or the Baseball Ground you'd get abuse, especially if you were winning or if you were causing their team problems. You had to be tough. That's been lost over the years. The modern grounds have lost a little bit of atmosphere. The crowd is the 12th man but you still get it at grounds like Hillsborough. Kenilworth Road is another compact ground for Luton. You can hear and feel that atmosphere, whereas the modern grounds lose that because the fans are further away. In those compact grounds the atmosphere can make you or break you. Sometimes before you can beat the team that you're playing you have to quieten the crowd. As the home team it makes a massive difference when you have a loud support. Highfield Road was a cocoon of a stadium, and once the crowd got behind you it was magnificent. The Highfield Road crowd shouting my name made me feel ten feet tall. But then if they started booing you they could make you feel two feet tall. You had to win them over and we started to do that as we put a good run together after losing the first game.

We went eight unbeaten, including a 3-0 win over Newcastle and a 1-0 against Watford in which I scored a goal in each. I made a really good start playing up front. You could see that the new style was working but we didn't know early on to what extent it would work. We were enjoying our football, though. When you go eight unbeaten people start looking at you. The media started talking about us. Typically, it was Aston Villa who ended that unbeaten run with a 1-0 defeat at Highfield Road. They scored a scrappy winning goal from Garry Thompson. We weren't happy because we were playing so well that we didn't expect to get beaten. But, it was a derby game and anything can happen. We had to recover from that and get back on track. We beat Rotherham in the League Cup next but then lost at Oxford before putting another mini run together of four unbeaten. We'd become a difficult side to play against, particularly at home. With that, the fans started to come back and attendances went up.

Just after Christmas we played Tottenham at Highfield Road and put in a magnificent performance in a 4-3 win. We had more than 22,000 fans there, which was double what we'd been getting earlier in the season, when we had just over 11,000 in the ground for the win over Watford in the September. I think that was when the fans started believing that this team could do something. As a player I started to think this was a good side. I didn't believe at that point that we'd go all the way in the cup but we were just doing the best we could to have a good season.

Our experience from previous seasons helped as well. There were still four or five of us who'd been there when we beat Liverpool under Bobby and were near the top of the table at Christmas of that season. We'd all seen that season that we slid down the table and ended up in a relegation battle, so just because we'd gone on a good run at the start of the 1986/87 season, we knew that we hadn't done anything yet. We were smarter by now as well. We had that mindset that if we couldn't win a game, we had to make sure we didn't lose it. We saw it that we started with a point, so made sure we left with at least a point. We'd learned how to manage a game by now. We could switch it when we needed to and we could recognise when we needed to change it, like we might defend a lead by playing it a little bit longer or switching it from playing to feet to getting down the channels to turn their defence. We had that experience so we knew what to do when we came into different situations.

We were playing to feet but if we needed to kick it into row Z we'd do that, we wouldn't keep the ball for the sake of keeping it. We were also solid at the back. Just because you play attacking football, that doesn't mean you can't be solid at the back. The passing football started from the back but we also defended from the front. The attackers worked hard and pushed and pressed and we kept our shape. We made it so that we were a difficult side to break down and we worked hard on that in training. Then, when we got the ball and broke we had those players like myself who could go at the opposition. We created so many chances from just winning the ball and then moving it quickly. That helped us have a good defensive record, and we'd only conceded 15 league goals by Christmas, compared to 35 at the same point the previous year.

It was a cold winter in 1986 and into 1987. We had some games called off due to frozen pitches so we ended up going away. We went to Bournemouth because we thought a little bonding session would help us, and it did. We went to No Man's Land. John knew the landlord of a pub there so we'd go there for a drink and play golf. That set us up nicely for the second half of the season. The lads enjoyed each other's company. Yes, you might have had little cliques and maybe some didn't always get on, but the unbelievable thing is that today, over 35 years later, that squad still meets up every few weeks. It's a unique relationship that we have and it goes to show the respect that John and George built up in that squad and also the character of the lads. We wanted to get on with each other, we wanted to do well for each other. If there was a fall-out, it was quickly forgotten. If there was a problem, we sorted it out ourselves and got on with it.

Sometimes a misunderstanding can be a good thing because we learned about each other from them. It was the same on the pitch; if there was a problem we didn't have to wait for half-time, we could change it ourselves on the pitch. We had the experience by then to be able to do that. John was very good at seeing things on the pitch but maybe we might see someone having a bit of a game and we needed to change it slightly to deal with it. If we were under the cosh slightly we might go man-to-man and you kept with your man so you quickly found out who it was who was causing the problem, which might be one of their players doing well or one of our own who wasn't quite doing his work. We'd say to him, 'Hey, sort this out and close it down quickly.' Like I've said, because we'd bonded we could do that to each other and it would be taken in the right way.

We had big characters who could take that; we had so many leaders. We had guys like Trevor Peake, Killer, Oggy, who were leaders. I was the same in a certain way. There are many ways of showing that you care. If I missed a chance it hurt so much but I had to keep my head up and look like I was happy or cocky. That was my way of doing it. Other lads might miss a chance and go in shouting and swearing and punching the doors. We all cared in our own way. We also spoke to each other in the right way, it wasn't like we were going, 'Hey you, you lazy whatever.' It was, 'Come on, he's having a bit of a game, sort it out.' You might not be having a good game but as long as you did your job then your team-mates would be happy. We all had each other's backs. We'd back each other and back each other, and then after the game probably take the mickey out of each other!

Another way that we'd change it on the pitch was that, under Sillett, in the first 20 minutes or so we'd play to feet. The centre-halves would think that was how we were playing and then we'd give the shout and we'd change the system and start going long. That just changed it up and rocked the defenders, suddenly we'd get it long into the channel. The centre-halves were then having to chase it. It worked brilliantly. We had that in our locker so that if it wasn't working early on we could change it up, and it worked for us.

Through this time we were just getting stronger and stronger. During the season we signed a lad called Dean Emerson. He joined us from Rotherham and was just what we needed. He liked to win the ball and gave another dimension to our team. John was always looking to develop the side and brought Dean in even though we were already doing well. Dean added to what we had and was a good player.

We had Bolton in the third round of the FA Cup and comfortably beat them 3-0. That could have been a banana skin because Bolton weren't a bad side and the pitch was a bit frosty. Those kinds of games are always difficult in the third round of the cup and at Coventry we had a habit of losing to lower league sides. Anything could happen in the cup so we knew that we had to be up for it and on it because if we weren't it could be the other team's day and they get a giant-killing. On days like that, things can just go against you. You might go for the ball one week and it drop right in front of you, and then the next week you go for the same ball and it drops a yard the other side of you. People look at that and think you look off the pace but some days you just don't get the bounce and things go against you.

On this day, though, Greg Downs scored a great goal and it set us on our way to winning it quite easily, much more easily than we thought, to be honest. We went in at half-time 3-0, I got a goal right on half-time, and John and George said to us that it wasn't 3-0, we were going back out for the second half as if it was 0-0. We had to have that mindset that it was 0-0, we needed to play the same and not take our foot off the pedal. If you're not up for it with the right attitude in the cup then you'll get turned over. Coventry had a reputation of not being very good starters in the cup so we were glad to make it through. We just took care of it professionally and then we went and drew Manchester United at Old Trafford in the next round. We couldn't have asked for a harder draw. Alex Ferguson had taken over by that point and when we played them at the end of January they were in the middle of a run in the league of one defeat in 13 matches, so we knew it was going to be a hard tie, especially as we were going to their place.

I was playing well, and then a setback; I got injured. I pulled a thigh muscle, which meant I missed league games against Arsenal and West Ham and then we went to Old Trafford. Because I was injured, Keith Houchen came in and did well at Man United. When we played Tottenham at Highfield Road, Keith scored a massive header. I had to watch on from the stands because of my injury and I thought we did well. We managed the game well. Keith did the business as he did in the cup with a goal. We scrapped it out.

I hated watching rather than playing. Obviously, I wanted the lads to do well but I just kept thinking about getting back fit. In my career I'd pretty much always been first choice and hadn't, at this point, had a lot of injuries. I just wanted to get fit and get back into the team. To see the lads win, though, that gave me even more incentive to get fit. I wanted to get back and be back in the side for the fifth round. Once we beat Man United people started to think maybe it was our year, but there was still a long way to go. But they say whoever beats Man United has a great chance of getting to Wembley. At this point, though, people started to look at us. John put belief into us and things started happening for us.

Someone who didn't have that belief in us was Jimmy Greaves, who tipped us to lose in every round of the cup. The lads would listen to that kind of thing and watch it, but you didn't take too much notice of it. I was one of those players who didn't like to watch myself on TV because I'd see things I thought I could have done better. Saint and Greavsie were just having a bit of banter but there was no doubt about it that we were getting more exposure in the media than we were used to.

There's pictures of us waiting around for the draw for the fifth round of the cup, and we drew Stoke. Away from home, yet again. I was back from injury but we had quite a few injuries and I ended up playing in midfield. Stoke were a decent side and that was one of the hardest games in the cup run. We went to their place and beat them 1-0. We had a little bit of luck as well because Stoke had a good shout for a penalty when Lee Dixon was brought down in the box. Stoke kept bombing at us, it was a difficult game. We rode our luck a couple of times that day. There was pressure in that match but don't forget we'd had a hell of a lot more pressure the three previous years having to win games to stay in the division. If we'd lost one of those games we knew we'd be relegated. If we lost against Stoke in the fifth round of the FA Cup it was different; of course we wanted to win but it wasn't that same kind of pressure.

That experience helped us managing games like that Stoke tie. That win was part of a six-game winning run in all competitions, which tells you how well we were doing at that time. By now we were really thinking, *You never know here, you never know.* Yet again, there were more and more eyes on us. This is again where John and George were so clever because they took us away again and got us out of the spotlight. It got us away from it all and we could just let off some steam.

That match was followed by wins in the league against Charlton and Sheffield Wednesday, and then we played Sheffield Wednesday again, this time in the FA Cup quarter-final; another away tie, of course. Back at Highfield Road at this time you could feel the mood changing in the ground compared to the season before. The atmosphere was electric. After Christmas you went out there to a full crowd. You could feel it, well, you didn't have to feel it, you could see it! Our away support was incredible as well, particularly in the cup. We'd walk out and you could see that the away section was full. The city was behind us. It wasn't just in the grounds, there was a different atmosphere when you went out in the city. The fans believed in it, the players were starting to believe in it but we still had to go out and prove we could do it. It was all set up for us to do something, it was now all about us going and doing it.

Something that helped was having a settled side. I think we only used 17 players. The players knew they'd be playing, they felt confident and we felt that the manager had confidence in us because he was picking the same team every week. It was a settled side, it wasn't players coming in and out every week. It created a side full of cohesion. Now that it's the quarter-final, you've got a few weeks between the fifth round and the quarter-final and the excitement is really building. It's all anyone is talking about. Our name is on the cup. It's all over the media. We know we're going to Sheffield Wednesday with a good chance. We've realised that, hey, we're not a bad team. We've had the big-match

A NEW ERA

experiences but they've played a lot of big games as well. They've been in the latter stages of cup competitions in recent years and it's going to be a hard match.

Even though it would be a hard match, we loved playing at Hillsborough. We always seemed to do well there. Even Oggy scored there one time! They were doing well at the time but so were we. We knew we had to get off to a good start, which we did. We scored a great goal, thanks to some great movement from Cyrille, to put us 1-0 up. We were doing just fine. They equalised and the crowd just went crazy. The roof came off the stadium, it was so loud. That's when you need your big players to step up. You've got your manager shouting from the sideline but that's when you need to manage the game as a group of players and really stand up. As a player you need to make the right runs, make the tackles and make the right decisions. We'd had the challenge of Man United, we'd had the challenge of Stoke, so the challenge we were facing here was something we could just take in our stride.

We were thinking of just hanging on and getting them back to Highfield Road for the replay. John got the No.10 board ready to sub Keith off, put me up front and get Micky Gynn or Dave Phillips out on the wing. As he did that, we knocked the ball up the front and Keith went on his left and made it 2-1. John quickly put that No.10 back! We ended up getting a lucky bounce from a clearance and Keith buried it to make it 3-1 to kill the game off. We were wondering what was going on. We'd gone to Sheffield Wednesday, which was a difficult place, and we more or less took them to pieces. That went hand in hand with how well we were playing in the league. We were getting the best out of myself and Cyrille and were a real unit. It was a happy squad with a happy atmosphere. Everyone was happy. We took 15,000 fans with us for that match, which was unbelievable. You don't get that sort of travelling support even now, it was phenomenal.

After the match there was us, Leeds, Watford and Spurs left in the cup. We wanted to draw Leeds because we thought they were the weaker side. We were waiting by the radio to hear who we'd got. We got our wish and drew Leeds, and would be going back to Hillsborough to play them. As it turned out, it was a harder game than we thought it would ever be.

On-pitch celebrations at Hillsborough after our FA Cup win against Leeds.

Gunning for glory at Wembley.

Celebrating with fellow goalscorer Keith Houchen.

Here we go! Celebrating my equaliser in the 1987 FA Cup Final.

Lifting the FA Cup with John Sillett.

Holding the FA Cup aloft with John Sillett and George Curtis.

All smiles ahead of a new season. Note the FA Cup Winners message above the club badge.

Back at Wembley for the 1987/88 Charity Shield.

Lining up with the 1987/88 Coventry squad.

Two tricky wingers battle for the ball. Coming up against John Barnes, August 1987.

A round of golf as part of our celebrations to mark 25 years since Coventry's FA Cup win. April, 2012.

All smiles on the pitch as Coventry play Swindon, March 2013.

On media duties during Coventry's FA Cup tie against Oxford, January 2024.

8

Here We Go

THERE WAS huge interest in tickets for the match. Highfield Road was packed because fans needed vouchers from league games for the cup ties. We played Oxford in March and beat them 3-0 in front of a full house. That match came at the end of six wins on the spin in all competitions. We were flying but then lost our next two, against Wimbledon and Villa, and drew 0-0 with Forest before the cup match against Leeds.

Keith was a lucky charm for us. He wasn't scoring in the league but kept scoring in the cup, so when it came to the cup he came into the side and I went back out to the wing, even though I'd been playing well up front with Cyrille. We did the same again in the semi-final against Leeds. That was the only change, really, that John had to make because we'd been playing well in the league. If you're struggling in the league but having a good cup run then the manager might want to tamper with things for a semi-final. John didn't have to.

The hardest thing for me was having to adapt my game just like that and switch from how I'd been playing up front all season to being back out on the wing. People don't realise how difficult that is. I didn't mind it, though, because I was doing a job for the team. I was doing really well as centre-forward but my first and foremost concern was that I was in the team. It was another string to my bow, I could play in either position. That was good for the manager as well, that he had that option. It was likely I could get a goal whether I was up front or out on the wing so the side still had that goal threat. It would have been naïve of John to have put Keith up front and take me out of the team altogether.

Because of how well we'd done all season, all of a sudden people were backing us to win. It was a Sunday lunchtime kick-off but because of the crowd congestion they put the kick-off back by half an hour. That wasn't ideal. You were focused ready to go out and then all of a sudden you've got to go back in and keep yourself mentally right. We were ready to walk out and had to go back in and get ourselves psyched up all over again.

They started like a house on fire and Oggy made some good saves to keep us in the game in the first ten or 15 minutes. They put us under so much pressure. They took the lead after 12 minutes through a David Rennie header from a corner. It took us a little bit of time to settle into the match and manage the occasion but then we probably should have gone in at half-time 3-2 up. Cyrille missed some great chances one-on-one. It shows his character that we went in 1-0 down and Cyrille was sat there in the corner. He was the big man and he sat there and said, 'Sorry, lads.' We told him not to say sorry. We gathered around him and told him we'd be alright and then, all of a sudden, Lloyd McGrath started singing. He was singing, 'Here we go, here we go, here we go.' Everyone started joining in. We were surprised that out of everyone in that dressing room it was Lloyd who was singing! God knows what Leeds were thinking because they were winning 1-0 in the semi-final of the FA Cup and here we were singing with our dressing room door open at half-time! That was the kind of character we had. We had a never-say-die attitude. We gave so much for each other.

Lloyd McGrath explains:

> I remember that day we had got ourselves all wound up for kick-off and then they delayed it. I was difficult to come back in and then have to get ourselves back up for it. We lost that bit of bite. We had to get the adrenaline going again.

I thought in the first half we were rubbish. I thought personally in the first half I was dreadful. It was Cyrille who said, 'Here we go,' and I just joined in and started singing. The rest of the lads joined in and I cannot describe the feeling, it filled us with energy. That was typical of that team that everybody joined in singing.

We went out there in the second half and gave it a real go. Midway through the half we were still 1-0 down and I chased a nothing ball down the wing and thought I had to make the tackle, I just wanted to keep the ball in play. The Leeds player, Brendon Ormsby, could have kicked the ball anywhere and I ended up sliding in right on the byline, getting it off him and keeping the ball in play. Once I'd done that, thank god I passed it to Lloyd. I don't think he's found his leg yet! He had a swipe at the ball and missed and it's ended up going to Micky Gynn, and he mis-kicked it and it's ended up in the net. Everything changed right then. If I'd been playing for Man United they'd still be showing that tackle every day! With that, I was getting the ball all the time and was causing all kinds of trouble. Micky Adams was smacking me all over the place. I was well up for it.

In these games you have to stand up, and I took it on myself to do something, whether that be beating a man or putting a cross in. I was just having that kind of game and that kind of season. That's not being cocky but that's how it was. It was just probably a surprise that one of the things that I did was putting a tackle in for the equaliser! As I went for the ball I knew I was going to get it, I just had to try and keep it in play. I saw Brendon a few years after and he told me the amount of stick he got for that because he could have just kicked the ball out or put it anywhere. Luckily, I got there and passed it, and thank god Lloyd missed it and we scored.

We went 2-1 up with a goal from Keith who I broke into the box, danced around the defenders and pulled it back to him. From the resulting ball in, the ball came back to Keith and he went around the goalkeeper and rolled it in. All we had to do was hang on. We thought that was it. But it's never over until the fat lady sings. Micky Gynn was chasing back in the corner and he got ragged off the ball by Andy Ritchie, and we still say to him to this day, 'What were you doing getting ragged by him?!' He crossed it and Keith Edwards headed it in, and the atmosphere blew the roof off again.

I said to Bugsy that we had to just make sure we didn't lose it. We weren't even sure on the pitch whether it would go to extra time or to a replay. It ended up in extra time. We were on the pitch in the break between full time and the start of extra time. John said I was having a bit of a game so he told the lads to get the ball out to me on the right wing and I'd make something happen. That showed how much he trusted me. John and George saw some players lying down and George went around telling everyone to stand up and not to let Leeds see that we were tired. They just went around giving each of us simple instructions for extra time. We knew we had it won and now had to do it all over again.

Moving into extra time, I was still having a bit of a game and was getting a lot of the ball down the right. I was getting at Micky Adams. I got to the byline again and he fouled me. As he fouled me I had cramp in my hamstring and limped away, wincing in pain with every step. We put the ball into the box and I was just walking in minding my own business and struggling with this cramp. The ball came in, Cyrille headed it down, Keith had a shot saved and it fell to me, and I just wanted to make a good contact. I smashed it in with my left foot and that won us the game. I couldn't even celebrate because the cramp in my hamstring was so painful. Everyone was running over to me and I was going, 'Ah, leave me alone, leave me alone!'

Then right at the end of the second half of extra time they broke and Oggy made another great save to keep it 3-2. The whistle went and it was just unbelievable. There's pictures of us dancing in front of the kop. The press wanted pictures of me, and I was saying, 'Yeah, that's fine, can I go now? Can I go now? I want to go celebrate with my lads!' I was happy to take all those plaudits but I was one of the lads and I wanted to be with them. We went into the changing room and the game was on TV. It had been shown live but with a delay so it was still playing by the time we got into the changing room. If someone asked me what my perfect game was I'd have to put that one up there. I was flying that day. The sixth round was special because I made the goal with a great move between myself, Lloyd and Cyrille, but the semi-final was even better. I helped get us back into the game, had a hand in the second and then scored the winner. That game has to be right up there with my best. What a performance, but like I always said, we hadn't done anything yet!

We had this magnificent journey home. I went to a pub I used to like called the Rose and Crown. They had a backroom that I used to go to. Val and Albert ran it there. I went there, got half a lager and pushed my way to the backroom. Everyone was going crazy. I had to leave. I couldn't even drink my half of lager because it was so manic there. I had to go home and have a lager there. You couldn't come down from it that whole day. You didn't really take it in until the next day and you saw the city and felt the excitement. What an atmosphere there was once we knew we were going to Wembley. But even with that we still had the league programme and we didn't want that to slip. You were playing for your place at Wembley and we wanted to finish as high as possible in the table. From then it was all about keeping your feet on the ground, not over-indulging in anything and just bubbling, but without bubbling over.

We were on this great run in the cup and often when a team does that the league form suffers. That didn't happen with us, we were still doing well in the league. Sometimes when you know you're going to Wembley the players might be worried about getting injured so they drop off, but even though we were a settled team, you knew you still had to perform because you were playing for your place in the final. We'd also worked so hard all season that we wanted to end well.

John and George kept us on the boil and ticking over. Training was good, we worked hard but enjoyed it. They kept that balance, though, of not working us too hard because we were playing midweek games as well. We played eight matches between 18 April and the final day of the season on 9 May. That included four games in the last week of the season. We didn't change anything with our routine. We'd still go to the Connexion for pre-match, set up and just do our thing. George was great at keeping our feet on the ground. He'd give you a clip around the ear if you weren't doing what you should be doing. He grounded us and that really helped us. John and George wouldn't let us get complacent and you could see that in our form towards the end of the season.

After the semi-final, we lost 2-0 against Luton but then we went seven unbeaten up to the end of the league season. We played Man United on the second to last home game in midweek and we had a full house, and then it was packed again three days later for the final league game of the season against Southampton. A 1-1 draw with the Saints ended the league campaign and we'd finished tenth. What a season it was. Finishing in the top half of the table and going to Wembley. What a turnaround it was in comparison to the previous few seasons. That form in the league helped us in the cup, helped us believe and gave us momentum. Winning is a habit, you can't just turn it on and off and it was a habit that we'd developed nicely that season. Then all that was left was the final itself. Well, there was actually plenty more going on in the week between the final game and the cup final. We had things like sorting out tickets for our parents and there was a lot of media stuff going on.

It was a great achievement for us to get to the cup final, but it goes back to what I said before, even though we'd done really well to get there, we hadn't won anything yet. For the final, the lads wanted Spurs because they were the bigger side. Tottenham were a bigger club than Watford and that would be a bigger cup final. We didn't mind too much, though, we were just pleased to be there. Some of the lads had never been to Wembley, never mind played in a cup final there.

The league games that we'd played between the semi and the final helped to take our minds off it a little bit but there was a lot of television interest. All of a sudden we were getting a lot of airplay from people like Saint and Greavsie. We were one of the top teams in the Midlands, crowds were up and the momentum was building very quickly. We had a players' pool and to put money into the pool we had to go out and do things for the club, events and things like that. I was out nearly every night because they wanted me and Cyrille. We went to Bournemouth, and while we were there me and Cyrille had to go and open some Barratt Homes! We got picked up in a Rolls-Royce, these two black guys being chauffeure around. It was crazy, there was so much going on in the run-up to the final. I was lucky because I'd been through it before from the final with Manchester City. It was different this time, though; now I was one of the main players because I'd had a good season and I was in demand to turn up for this and that. I had to be everywhere. It kept my mind busy, though, kept my feet on the ground and probably boosted my popularity a bit.

Something else that we did was record the cup final song. Of course, it's this tradition and Spurs had a hit with one so of course we had to do one. We went to somebody's house to record it. It was a house in Kersley. The lads were getting the sheets and singing it and we were wondering what we were doing singing this song in someone's front room. The song was 'Go for It' and we wanted to match Tottenham. They had Waddle and Hoddle so me and Cyrille did a bit together in the song. Some of the lads weren't into singing but they knew we had to do a song. It was part and parcel of the cup final. We were a good group and up for a laugh so everyone joined in. We warmed to it pretty quickly. We were pleased with how it came out even if we were surprised we were recording in someone's house. We went in and recorded it and then had a game on the Saturday, and then we went back in again to finish it off.

We could only do all these media things because we were playing well in the league. If we'd been losing games then John would have had us back in training and working on things, but he knew he could trust us to perform on the pitch so we were fine. Despite all this stuff around the cup final, we knew we had to be on it for Saturday and John made sure that we were on it for every match. You knew that if you didn't watch yourself or got out of line, then you might not be playing in the cup final.

Then we went on *Blue Peter*. When we got there, we arrived late. We were supposed to be there from 10am and there for most of the day rehearsing. We turned up at about 3pm, and we were going on air at 5pm! They got us to run through what we were going to do. We had to sing the song. We were singing it pretty flat, 'Go for it, go for it, City.' The editor came out and asked us what we were doing. She said, 'You can't sing it like that, you've got to sell yourself on this programme. You've got to sell the song.' Killer said maybe if they got the lads a drink it would be alright. So they went out and got us 48 cans of lager. We went downstairs into the changing room and drank these 48 cans of lager. By the time we came back up to do the show we were screaming, 'GO FOR IT, GO FOR IT, CITY!' We really went for it. That was the lads. Brilliant. If you watch that clip you can see that the lads were singing it half-cut.

We went into the final with a couple of players missing. Dean Emerson had done well in midfield since coming in but picked up an injury ahead of the quarter-final and had been ruled out for the season. Brian Borrows picked up an injury in the last game of the season against Southampton. That was a massive blow. He did his knee in a tackle. It was tragic for Bugsy, we all really felt for him. Bugsy had been a regular for a good while and he probably would have been the first name on the team sheet at Wembley. John trusted the players that he had, though. Dave Phillips had played at right-back before so we didn't have to change our style because of the injury. They had good players like Clive Allen, who had scored 48 goals already that season, and of course they had Hoddle and Waddle. Lloydy was given the job of sticking with Hoddle but he was also given the job of sticking with Waddle, so he was working hard. We didn't change too much, we wanted to put our game on to their game. They played with just one up front and we thought Peakey was capable of handling Clive Allen, and then we had Oggy as well, so we were strong at the back.

After playing Southampton in the final match we went to Bournemouth, came back on the Tuesday and the youth team were playing in the FA Youth Cup Final on the Wednesday, so we went to watch them. The lads got new cars from Peugeot on Thursday and we went to our hotel, the Compleat Angler, on the Friday. That was on the Thames and we stayed there overnight. We had a few lagers there on the Friday night. We were going to have a few drinks on that Friday night wherever we were. We went for a walk after our dinner and went over the bridge into Marlow. As we went over the bridge we passed an off-licence so we went in and got a few cans. We probably had three or four cans each. We went back through the hotel reception and the concierge saw us walking in with bags full, and some of them going ching, ching. He went and told John Sillett. John trusted us and said to leave us alone to have a drink because we had the biggest game of our lives the next day and we needed to relax our nerves. He shot him down! He probably thought he was going to get us into trouble and get himself a pat on the back, and he got shot down. It backfired on him. We went upstairs, had a game of cards, *Cheers* was on the TV, and we relaxed. We made our phone calls for tickets. I had new boots that I had to soak and we had a few drinks, obviously. I could have had a load of drinks and still played the same the next day. You had a lager or two just to settle the nerves.

Something that John did to help us, something that you shouldn't do, is he paid the groundsman at Wembley so we could train on the pitch. That was a big help because so many of the side had never played there before. Having been there before, I knew the stadium, the changing rooms, the baths, so I could speak to the lads and tell them what it was like in the build-up. On the day it's completely different. You get there and you're probably a bit more prepared than you would be for any other game. This is it. This is your time. This is what you've been thinking about for all these weeks. You have a bit of a rehearsal of what happens in the line-up when a member of the royal family walks down the line, because when that's finished you get a signal and then break away, so we had a rehearsal of that. You had to be ready for 2.45pm rather than the usual 3pm.

When you get out there on the pitch it doesn't matter how prepared you are, being out there on that pitch is completely different. You know you've got people in 60 different countries all over the world watching, there's 100,000 inside the stadium and then all of those people at home. I made some comparisons between that day and the final that I'd lost with Man City but you can't think about that too much. The Duchess of Kent walked down, being introduced to the teams before kick-off in the royal line-up. She said something to a few of the lads. When she got to me she said, 'It's because of you that you're here today, isn't it?' I smiled and said yes.

I just wanted to get the game started. My mind was racing. I didn't want to let anyone down. We had parents there, friends, family, everyone who knows you is watching. This was it. This is what we'd dreamed about and played all season for and now here we were. At the same time you didn't want to be over-emotional but you did want a few nerves. It was the game of our lives. I wasn't as on edge as I was in 1981 but at the same time you still feel that pressure of the unknown, you didn't know what was about to happen. By the end of the match someone was going to be a hero and it might be someone you wouldn't expect. The biggest players in the world have gone out at Wembley and frozen. Big teams have frozen at Wembley. The biggest game of my life was about to kick off against a Tottenham side that had never lost in a final at Wembley. But it was like John Sillett said, we'd never lost in a final at Wembley either, but that was because we'd never been in one!

I just wanted to get out there and get an early touch of the ball and get settled. Getting a feel of the ball early on was important. Tottenham had never lost a cup final. We'd never been there. Everyone fancied Tottenham. We were going there thinking we had a great chance. We'd beaten them 4-3 in the league so we were thinking, *Hey, we're alright!* Everyone was writing us off just because they had loads of internationals but we had a good side as well. John said to us before we went out to not give away an early goal. Well, within two minutes Clive Allen scored to make it 1-0. So much for not giving away an early goal.

I remember Cyrille saying to me, 'Benno, let's just keep the score down.' I said, 'Just let me get a kick of the ball!' We kicked off and we got back into it after nine minutes. The ball went into the box and Keith flicked it on. Because I'd been playing centre-forward, I was able to come in from the wing and get into the middle because I could double up as an extra forward in the box. That gave us an extra goal threat. I read the flick from Keith and, as I got there, I got in front of Mitchell Thomas. I took the ball around Ray Clemence, who caught me with his studs as I went around him, and then it was just about balancing myself as I took the shot. He clipped me but all I was thinking about was scoring. I had a chance to score in the FA Cup Final and I wanted to score, not go down for a penalty. I'd scored all these important goals, so trying to score was what came naturally to me.

Afterwards, if I'd missed, I probably would have thought I should have gone down, won us a penalty and maybe got Clemence sent off. But at the time I was just thinking of scoring. There was someone on the line and I didn't think about missing, I just thought about hitting the back of the net, which I did. I did it in one movement. When that ball hit the net, that feeling, wow. The lads came and grabbed me and it wasn't like a pat on the back to say congratulations, it was a grab as if to say, 'We're back in the game.' It was the chains being released and they just hugged and grabbed me. I didn't even have time to celebrate. We needed that goal. You could feel it. You could feel the relief. That feeling will stick with me for as long as I live.

As I turned away and ran back to the halfway line to get into position, I thought, *Yes, I've scored but I've still got a job to do.* We were back in the game. With that, the lads got confident, I got confident and we could start playing. It was one of the most important goals I've ever scored in my life because we needed to score when we did. We took responsibility on the pitch and put it right after such a bad start. We were back level but then found ourselves behind at half-time when Gary Mabbutt scored on 41 minutes. It was up to the manager then to do something during the break. He had a bit of a go at Greg and told him to get closer to Waddle.

Greg smashed Waddle in the first few minutes of the second half with a tackle and set the tone for the team. I wanted to get back into the game and was doing the best I could to influence it. We'd played just over an hour and Keith laid the ball out to me. As the ball came to me, Keith turned and sprinted into the box. The natural thing for me to do was to cross the ball. If I'd been playing up front I'd want the winger to cross it first time. I was trying to give them the service that hopefully they'd have given to me. I whipped it in and, of course, Keith threw himself at it and scored this fantastic goal. I'd have taken any goal at that point, tap-in, header, 30-yard screamer, but for Keith to score a diving header like he did, it was a dream come true, as he recalls:

> I've teased Benno a lot over the years, saying that was the only good cross he put in during my three

years at Coventry. He was great, though, and that was just what he could do. That's why it all worked, because I knew I could set off and gamble because Benno could beat someone and get the ball in. He had such quick feet. That day at Wembley, he just took it to one side and whipped it in. If someone did that now they would show it over and over and over. The ball does it for you nowadays, it curves on its own. In our day it took a lot of skill and technique to bend the ball like that.

I've talked Benno's goal up a lot over the years as well. He says to me he's sick of my goal because everyone forgets that he scored one! His was such a great goal though. I glanced it on, he took it around the keeper and, as you look at it as a goalscorer, if he had just hit that straight away the lad on the line would have blocked it. Benno looked up and deliberately played it behind the defender and into the part of the net that the defender had come flying in from. It was a really clever goal. He was the only one who would have scored that goal because he had to think faster than everyone else and then have such quick feet to get around the goalkeeper and score. You work hard for 20 years and sometimes it all comes together on one day and for us it all came together on that one day.

Greg Downs:

The second goal at Wembley was typical of Dave, he got his half a yard and got the ball into the box and Houchen knew it was coming in. Houchen anticipated it because he knew Dave would get the ball in early. Dave scored and made a lot of goals that season. He was one of the main reasons that we had a good season. Dave was one of those characters where when things were going well he was pretty much unplayable. He had great feet, he could get half a yard and when he was on his game he was one of the best wingers in the league.

We were back in it once again. We regrouped and said to each other we had to manage it and not give anything away. We had a couple of chances to win it in 90 minutes but we ended up in extra time. John and George saw us sitting down and, just like in the semi-final, they got us all on our feet to not show Spurs that we were tired. John said to get the ball out to me and I'd make things happen from the right wing.

The story is that on 96 minutes the ball came out to Lloyd on the right wing, and John thought it was me. When he realised it was Lloydy, he said, 'What's he doing out there?!' Lloydy can't even cross his legs to save his life but somehow he put this cross in and it deflected off Gary Mabbutt and went in. It was unfortunate that it was an own goal but we took it. We'd finally got ourselves in front and we felt we couldn't lose it now, we had to get over the line.

The final whistle blew. We'd won the FA Cup. Everyone was celebrating on the pitch. I got plenty of attention and plaudits for my performance from the fans, the media and even the opposition.

David Pleat (Tottenham manager):

> We knew Cyrille was good in the air and he had done well against Richard Gough previously. We thought they might detail Micky Gynn to mark Glenn but we couldn't be sure. We changed our team quite a bit before the final to protect players. Coventry played Leeds in the semi and weren't the favourites then. Coventry supporters probably thought their name was on the cup. There was that story as well about the players

seeing a wedding on the day of the final. I've never watched the game back in all the years since, but what I can definitely say is that Dave Bennett played very well. He held sway over our left-back. I didn't realise the authority that he had over Mitchell Thomas until afterwards. It wasn't until after that I realised what a crucial area of the field that had been, where Bennett was staying wide and getting his crosses in. He made the difference.

Tottenham went up for their medals. As they came down we were waiting for ours. As they came down I waited and shook every one of their hands because it was redemption for me after losing in the final with Man City. I was one of the last up the steps to get my medal. After that I had to do a press conference. There was a guy called Mike Langley who wrote for the *Daily Mirror*. Before the game he said the only people who'd know the Coventry players were their families because they were nobodies. When I went into the press conference I asked for him, but surprisingly he wasn't there. By the time I got back to the changing room after that all my stuff had gone. My shirts and everything were gone. All I had left was what I had on me. That was disappointing.

We went back out after that and went up to the gantry because Jimmy Hill was doing *Match of the Day* and all he'd dreamed about was seeing his team at Wembley and all of us singing his song, 'Play Up Sky Blues'. All I wanted to do was see my family. Me, Cyrille and Micky Gynn walked out and at the top of the stand at the far end it said Tottenham 2 Coventry City 3. We just looked at it and said, 'Look at that, not bad at all.' We got on the coach and found out that vice-chairman Ted Stocker had put £1,000 on us to win the cup earlier in the season at 50/1, so we thought we might be in for a few bob.

At the start of the season we'd signed a contract about bonuses. It had listed every round of the cups and how much bonus you'd get. Because Coventry City had never been anywhere near the final of a cup, the bonuses were nothing to what Tottenham were getting. I think Tottenham were on £17,000 a man just for appearing in the final, let alone to win it. We were on £2,000 or £3,000, nothing compared to Tottenham. The club made a lot of money out of it with ticket sales and everything. They made a lot of money and we made nothing, jack shit really. That was a bit disappointing, with what we'd just achieved. As daft as it may sound, though, money wasn't everything, we'd just won the FA Cup and we were happy. We thought maybe we'd get our reward the next season with new contracts on a bit more money. I was hoping for a bit more money because I'd been there five or six years now and was ready to be rewarded.

It wasn't until the next day when you saw it all in the papers that we realised that not only had the players achieved something, Coventry City had achieved something. They could never take that away from us or from the club. I was an FA Cup winner. FA Cup finals are often cagey, boring affairs because of the nerves and no one wants to put a foot wrong. That early goal meant that our final was never going to be boring. Put it this way, you couldn't put the kettle on! It was a magnificent game to have played in. To end up on the winning side of an FA Cup Final that was as entertaining as that one was a double bonus. I thought we deserved to win it as well. We played better than Tottenham, we had better chances. Once we got back to 2-2 I thought we were the stronger side and there was only one team that was going to win it, and that was us.

At 9am on the Sunday morning we went and picked Bugsy up from hospital so he could join in with the celebrations. That was us, a team on and off the park. We had a long, long, long day of celebrating. We were celebrating because finally we'd achieved something.

9
Shopping in Harrods

WE WENT into the new season full of confidence and ready to push on. John Sillett came out with a famous quote in the close season that finally Coventry City could shop in Harrods rather than Woolworths. We were an up-and-coming team, so when players were becoming available they'd look at Coventry City as a team that they wanted to come to. We were becoming one of the top teams. We played a good style of football, we carried ourselves well and were doing well. John suddenly had some money and we'd become a place where players wanted to come to.

John was thinking now about rotating the squad a little bit but we looked at it slightly differently. The lads thought we still had plenty of life in that side. Sometimes you do need to freshen up a team but we didn't think that was the case with this side at that point in time. Sometimes a manager thinks they need new players and they bring them in and then in training see that actually the new lads aren't as good as the ones he already had. Everyone in that cup-winning side was hungry to keep going and keep playing. We wanted to stick together. Freshening things up doesn't have to mean buying new players. You can freshen things up by bringing new staff in or by changing the tactics, it's not just buying new players. We still had a good squad, with guys like Steve Sedgley, Graham Rodger and David Smith coming through, and we had that strong backbone to the team.

We ended up bringing in David Speedie as the only signing that summer. Signing one good player with the money we had was a better move than signing five or six average players who wouldn't improve the side. He was a great lad and a really good player. He was really good in the air and we changed our game a little bit to supply him with the ball in the air. He brought another dimension to the team. He was very fiery, in more ways than one. He was like that on the pitch. He was very passionate with a capital P and in inverted commas! Off the pitch, he was a lovely lad. He always wanted to have a laugh, he was a joker. Sometimes his jokes went a little bit too far and he had to be reined in a little bit.

We were a group, so if anything ever happened that went over the line, we'd sort it between ourselves. That was the beauty of having good professionals like Trevor Peake and Cyrille. Any problems that cropped up were dealt with in-house. Players weren't cast aside, everything was dealt with. It was the same with any disagreements. We were 20 guys in that squad from different walks of life, different backgrounds, different senses of humour and you're not all going to get along all the time. You might get a few tasty tackles in a five-a-side and you wonder what's going on. No matter what it was, you dealt with it in-house, you knew each other inside out and you moved on.

Expectations were up. Fans were expecting more and so were the players. As players, our expectations had changed; we wanted to be winning, to play in front of big crowds, to get the praise on the TV. We'd reached a higher standard and we wanted to maintain those standards. Getting there was one thing but we wanted to stay there. We wanted another cup run and high finishes in the league. All of a sudden we were competing instead of battling at the bottom of the table. Fans can start to get a little bit spoilt when that happens and they get used to you taking on these big sides and winning. We wanted to keep on winning, but if you want the best things in life then you need to work hard for them and that comes on and off the pitch.

Off the pitch, you need to make sure you prepare in the right way. We were preparing well but that wasn't shown in the results in pre-season. It's not all about results in pre-season. The manager will be looking for the right combinations, players are still getting fit and getting into a rhythm and the feel of the ball again. There's a lot of aspects to it. We had a bad result, though, when we went and lost against Poole. You don't take it to heart in pre-season but, of course, ideally you'd like to be winning. It's the first game of the season that you need to be ready for, though, not the pre-season games. When you go and play Poole or a side like that they'll be giving it 100 per cent, tackling through you and running through brick walls because they're playing a top-flight side. You've got to look after yourself in games like that and avoid picking up an injury. The manager will always say to look after yourself in those games. You'd rather take a loss, even against a non-league side, and come through it unscathed than win and pick up injuries.

One disappointment was that despite winning the FA Cup we weren't playing in Europe because it came at a time when English clubs were banned. Not being in Europe was a massive blow. We deserved to be in Europe. It would have set the club up in more ways than one.

Before the league season started we were back at Wembley for the curtain-raiser that's the Charity Shield. Everton had won the league the previous season so they were the opponents. We were back at Wembley showing people that we were a team to be reckoned with. The Charity Shield was a big game. It was the best versus the best from the previous season. It was a big occasion for us and the fans, a trip back to Wembley for them. We had fans who'd missed the FA Cup Final but could make it to the Charity Shield. Not many players get the chance to play at Wembley so you had to respect the game and occasion as it was an honour for us to go back to Wembley.

People might not see the Charity Shield as a big game but I did; hey, I wish I was playing in another one now! It was different to the FA Cup, though; the pressure was still there to win but it was different because we'd already won the cup. It was a nice sunny day and that intensity of the cup final wasn't there. Some of the lads had never been to Wembley when we got to the cup final and now here we were again, so the squad wasn't as tense when it came to this one. We still wanted to go down there and enjoy the occasion, though. As for the game itself, I thought we should have won it over the 90 minutes. We lost 1-0, Wayne Clarke scored the winner just before half-time in front of 88,000 fans. Bugsy missed the cup final, of course, but came on for the last few minutes as a sub for Micky, so he at least got to step out at Wembley in a Coventry shirt.

Even though we lost, we were going into the season knowing that we could do something. We weren't candidates to go down like we had been a year earlier. The betting odds had been turned upside down. We were going into the season thinking we could get into the top six. We had real firepower and some money behind the club. Things were looking good. We'd had one hell of a turnaround in a year. The feeling of going into a season when everyone was looking at Coventry City and we weren't relegation fodder anymore, it was unbelievable. We weren't even thinking about relegation anymore.

People were looking at some of the players for England caps around this time. The England manager was looking at four or five Coventry City players for inclusion in the England squad; that was massive. Looking back, I think there should have been more international recognition for the players in that squad. Maybe not for everyone to get caps but we should have been in the squad. We had some good English players who were playing well. Maybe it was because we were playing for Coventry City. When you're playing for a so-called smaller club they might want you to prove yourself for another season in comparison to someone playing for a bigger club. Guys like myself, Peakey, Oggy, Cyrille, Bugsy; to have England managers thinking of picking us was a testament to how far we'd come. We were thinking that if we started the season well, then with a word here and there we might just get the recognition of an England call-up.

Bobby Robson, the England manager at that time, came to watch us in the first game of the season. After the match, John Sillett came in and told me that Bobby Robson had been watching me. I didn't think I'd had the best of games. I did well but I possibly didn't do enough. After that, the right-wing spot tended to go to David Rocastle or Neil Webb. We knew that we were being watched and it was nice to be told but I just didn't quite get selected. It would have been nice to have made a squad, the same for Oggy, Bugsy and Peakey. It would have been nice for the club, the fans and, of course, for ourselves.

Steve Ogrizovic:

> People talk about unfashionable clubs, and maybe that was a factor [in Coventry players not playing for England] but it's nice for people to mention us as having an opportunity for England. Dave deserved that for his performances, especially in the cup run in '87 and his performance in the final.

As well as having the England manager in the crowd, the match was notable as it pitted the cup finalists against each other on the opening day. The match was at Highfield Road, but as we were playing Spurs, unbelievably, it was decided that we couldn't have the trophy there because it might cause problems. Imagine that, the only time we've ever won it and we can't even parade it! We must be the only team to not parade the FA Cup on the opening day of the following season. There's probably a quiz question about that one! If it had been the other way around and Spurs won the FA Cup, then they'd have paraded it. I thought it was a bit out of order that wewere denied that.

We had a big crowd, Highfield Road was packed and it would have been nice to have paraded the cup after the game. The crowd could have stayed behind to see the cup. That would have avoided problems of us parading it before the game and upsetting Spurs and their fans. That was an occasion that our fans should have been able to enjoy. It was thought that Tottenham might think we were rubbing their noses in it. So what? They shouldn't have lost the game then, should they?! If we did it after the game the Tottenham players and fans would have been on their way home by the time we did it. Even without the cup, we beat Spurs on the opening day. They'd have been thinking about getting a bit of revenge after the cup final but we went and got a 2-1 win, with Speedie scoring on his league debut.

We then beat Luton but lost against Norwich and Liverpool. A few weeks later we lost 3-0 against Forest. Those defeats didn't get us down at all. We just knew that we had to start working a bit harder and get the performances in. From October we went on a bad run where we lost six in a row and then drew the next five. The thing was, in almost all of the games they were very tight. The defeats were usually by one goal. We were giving it a go, we weren't just lying down and getting beaten. The fans will stick with you through bad patches like that when they can see that you're putting in a shift.

The pitch was bad that year and had to be sanded; that didn't help us. We had injuries, like Lloyd breaking his leg. All of this has to be taken into account. We were used to having a very balanced team so we needed to adjust to changes and get used to the pitch. The manager could see that we were almost there but we just weren't getting that little luck of the bounce and we were losing close matches. He just had to keep faith in us and we kept faith in him. We lost 3-1 against Newcastle in that run and Paul Gascoigne had a good game, which was rare because Lloydy usually handled him. Lloydy always had Gazza, he hardly ever had a good game against us. I'd say nine out of ten times we kept Gazza quiet, but unfortunately not on that day. Lloydy was fantastic in that job. Gazza was such a talented player and Lloydy kept him quiet and man-marked him again and again.

The big disappointment from that season was going out of the FA Cup in the fourth round against Watford. We'd beaten Torquay 2-0 in the third round and drew Watford at home. It was snowing that day, raining, everything. It wasn't an easy day to play but we fancied our chances and thought we'd go on another good cup run. That defeat hurt a lot more than losing to Liverpool or Forest in the league. That was a blow, to be knocked out early on, especially at home. The season before we'd been the underdogs almost every round but at home to Watford we fancied it. We did well in the game. Trevor Senior came off the bench to score the only goal in front of a near-full house at Highfield Road. Put it this way, the players weren't happy about being beaten at home, and the gaffer certainly wasn't happy.

We had to have a look at ourselves after that match. The dressing room stayed calm afterwards, though. The manager came in and, as he would, said bits and pieces, but then we'd always have the inquisition on a Monday morning when John had calmed down and maybe seen the game again. Instead of going through it all when everyone was still hyped up on the Saturday, he'd save it for Monday. He'd still say a few things right after the game but would go into more detail on the Monday. After a defeat like that we'd drown our sorrows in the best way possible. We'd go out, have a drink, talk about the game and then go in on Monday ready for a week of hard work to make sure you put it right and bounced back. On the Monday you'd go through Saturday's game and have a loosener, Tuesday he'd work you hard and then Wednesday and Thursday was getting everything set for the next match.

Goals were hard to come by early that season despite the attacking talent that we had with Cyrille and Speedie. It took them a little while because Speedo was a different kind of centre-forward. He'd win things in the air and flick the ball on. Cyrille always wanted the ball to his feet so it took some time for it all to click. Maybe we should have stayed as we were. I'd been enjoying playing up front and I was put back out on the wing. We changed the formation a little and it's like moving into a new house, you change things slowly, you don't go decorating every room at the same time. Speedo was a great player but bringing him in meant that we had to change. Signing a great player doesn't necessarily always work. We were adapting a system that had worked well for us and brought us some success. Speedo did well for us and finished top scorer that season but it took some work from everyone. I think John would admit that we had to change our style for him to fit in.

We may have made an early exit from the FA Cup, but one cup we did have a good run in that year was the Simod Cup, where we got to the semi-final. With any tournament, the further you go, the bigger it gets. We reached the semi-final, so all of a sudden it was a big deal and a way for us to get back to Wembley. The Simod Cup wasn't the biggest competition but we wanted to get to Wembley, and when you get there it doesn't matter what competition it is, you want to win it. People remember winners. If we'd lost in 1987, who would remember us? We played Reading in the semi-final and lost on penalties. I always say now to not let a game get to penalties. We had good penalty takers but on the night some of them didn't want the responsibility. They didn't fancy it. John told them that they needed to step up to the plate.

You've only got one nominated penalty taker, so when you get to a shootout and you need five or more penalty takers, you'll only have a few of those players who have ever practised taking penalties. But the strikers often miss more than the defenders in shootouts. The strikers have added pressure that people expect them to score, whereas the defenders just pick their spot and don't worry about it. Strikers stay behind after training to practise them and pick their corners and might overthink it in a shootout. You don't see many defenders staying behind to practise their penalties, so they just go up and smack it in. If it's a World Cup or a big competition like that, then teams might expect penalties and practise. Let me tell you, we weren't looking at the Simod Cup like the World Cup! I missed and we lost 4-3. When you're standing on the halfway line you need to have decided what you're going to do. What happens, though, is you're standing there and you watch the goalkeeper dive the same way for all the other penalties and you were planning on putting it that way, so it puts doubt in your mind. You end up walking from the halfway line with doubts, and you change your mind. That's what happened and since then I never changed my mind when taking a penalty.

We'd had a sticky patch in the league and there's no secret to how you turn it around when you're on a bad run, it was just hard work. Things picked up around February and suddenly we were flying again. We got revenge for the FA Cup by beating Watford in the league 1-0, and from February only lost two in 13. We were on a great run and then we came up against Derby on 19 March 1988. It would be a game that I'd never forget, but not for the right reason. We lost the match 3-0 and I collided with Peter Shilton and broke my leg. I did my shin on his head. It was a 50-50 challenge. During my Man City days, I had a coach called Dave Ewing who said goalkeepers would always come out and protect themselves, and they'd do you. Dave would say that in a 50-50 with the goalkeeper you always go and do the goalkeeper because the goalkeeper would do you, so look after yourself and do the goalkeeper. If you do the goalkeeper you have a great chance of winning because they didn't have sub goalies in those days!

That was drilled into my mind. I knew Shilton would be coming to do me but unfortunately I came off worse. I went into it thinking I want to win 51 per cent of this and he can have 49. I went into his head and limped off the pitch. I didn't know I'd cracked the tibia until later that night. It was painful straight away but I didn't realise how bad it was. A few minutes after it happened the pain got more intense. I tried to carry on but was limping. I did well to walk off the pitch. No disrespect to the club, but they could have got into big trouble because they didn't check me out there and then and allowed me to go home. They didn't send me for an X-ray. I went home and was in pain at home, the pain was excessive. I was lucky to not make it worse when I got home. I knew I was in trouble when I went to come down the stairs on my bum after going to the toilet. I knew something was wrong. I went straight to the hospital.

I was blessed that Lloyd had recently broken his leg as well so I had someone to work with and try to catch up to him. Lloydy is a keep fit machine. They always used to say you had to do what Lloydy did, and believe me you couldn't do what Lloydy did! I was determined to just get back. I went to Lilleshall and it was hard work. The pain was intense. I couldn't do anything for the first few weeks so that time was just to get used to the pain. I'd have my foot elevated so the blood would rush down when you got up and the pain was incredible. I wouldn't wish that pain on anyone. It was a fracture so they plastered me up to my thigh. I had a couple of weeks in a full-length cast and then I had a fibreglass plaster up to my knee. I could still go into training and do upper-body work and I'd do lots of sit-ups. I had to keep working on the top of my leg as well because when you're in plaster you lose the muscle at the top of the leg, so I had to keep building that up.

Lloyd McGrath:

> My first impression of Dave was that he was a larger-than-life character. When you first saw him you thought, *Oh no, this one could be trouble.* As you got to know him you realised he was such a down-to-earth lad. He was someone who was always there willing to help you. We helped each other when we were both coming back from broken legs. It can be lonely coming back from an injury but we had each other to help each other

along. I was quite a fit lad and I used to try and push Benno to the limits. To be fair to him he used to keep up with me. We used to go on bike rides and at first I'd be miles ahead of him but then eventually he'd be right behind me. We used to have a right laugh while getting ourselves fit; if you don't laugh then it can become depressing. We got each other through it.

I was in every day of the week, no day off because I wanted to get back fit. I was in morning and afternoon. I'd see the lads around all the time because I was at the training ground when they came in. I'd be watching the games as well. I was still interacting with the lads but was training a lot more than they were until I could get back out on to the grass. It's good to be around the players when you're out for a long time like I was. Your mindset when you're injured is different because you're no good to the club when you're injured, so you just want to get back fit. It was difficult to see new players coming in and playing in my position. Someone had to play there, though, and it couldn't be me so I had to just take it as a challenge. The first challenge was getting myself fit. Once I got fit then I could face the challenge of winning my place back. I couldn't hold any grudges, I wanted the lads to do well, so I wanted whoever was playing in my position to do well. I wanted them to do well so I could come back into a winning side. I didn't want to come back to a losing side; you could end up coming back to a relegated side. You had to support the lads and want them to win.

However, I was disappointed because I think I'd scored seven goals that year, and if I scored ten I'd get a bonus. I was coming up for a new contract as well, and this is where things turned a little bit sour. I was offered a four-year contract and they took me down to a three-year one because maybe they thought I wasn't going to be the player I was before the injury. I was a bit peed off by that because what happened to loyalty? I'd gone through bad times and good with the club and I was expecting them to reward me and look after me a little bit more than they did. I was a little bitter about it.

Different players were brought in to replace me because I was out for nine months. I had to concentrate on getting fit so I could get back into the team and show them that not only was I better than the players they'd brought in but also that I was going to be the player that I'd been before. The contract talks dragged on while I was injured. I wanted this four-year contract but they'd only give me three years. I wasn't looking to go anywhere else and I thought I deserved that contract. I wasn't quite into my 30s at that point and still had a lot to offer. I was still a first-team player and thought I was at Coventry City to stay. I was one of the first on the team sheet. I wanted that four-year deal but I took the three-year contract that they were offering in the end. I thought I'd see where it took me and I was already thinking about a testimonial.

The new deal wasn't much of an increase on what I'd been on before. If I hadn't got the injury and had got an England call-up then money might have changed, but it didn't happen. It would have been better for me financially to have been a two-bob player who bounced around from club to club. I had six years as an important player in a good Coventry team but I'd have made more money as a journeyman going from transfer to transfer, getting a signing-on fee each year. At the time, you earned more money like that than being a good player who signed on a three-year contract.

* * *

I was out for nine months which took us into the 1988/89 season. We ended the 1987/88 season tenth, the same as the year before, which was another good season for us. I came back at the start of 1989. Once you've had an injury like I had then it's always in your mind because you think it could happen again. You have that worry when you go down after a tackle because you'll always have a little bit of a weak spot there and you're more protective about it. Don't forget, we were playing in an era where you could still get tackled from behind. I had to try to put it behind me and push on.

I came back in a match against Sheffield Wednesday at Highfield Road on 2 January 1989. Myself and Lloydy were both back in the team after suffering broken legs and there was a lad in the Wednesday team called Ian Knight who was making his first appearance after breaking his leg. Cyrille was returning from injury as well. Speedo scored a hat-trick of headers and we won 5-0. That game was on the Monday and we had Sutton United in the FA Cup third round on the Saturday. I'd played well against Sheffield Wednesday and got through the game but my recovery wasn't quite right. The Sutton game might have come too quickly for me and I should have eased back into the team. I'm not using that as an excuse for what happened against Sutton, though. We built up to it as a normal game, despite the fact that we were playing a non-league side and we were heavy favourites. Obviously, you had things like the changing rooms were smaller and it was a bit different getting into the ground but we treated it like any other game. We knew what we were there for and we were on it, or so we thought.

For Sutton, it was one of the biggest games they were ever going to play. They were up for it, running for everything, going into every challenge. The message for us before the kick-off was to just go and play our usual game. The thinking was if we did that we'd have enough to win it. We went out there and they got the first goal just before half-time and it changed it all. The mentality of the game changed. They were getting little bits of luck, they were winning the 60-40 balls. We were creating chances and then missing them. We were hitting the woodwork, they were blocking things on the line and you start thinking it isn't going to be your day. We went in at the break 1-0 down.

At half-time John said to just keep on going. We were making chances. We hadn't done much wrong and we knew Sutton would get tired and chances would come for us. We just needed a goal and how we got it didn't really matter. We just carried on playing and wanted to keep knocking on the door. We kept knocking but the door wouldn't open. But, eventually we equalised seven minutes into the second half thanks to a Dave Phillips goal. We had improved so much in managing games over the years and realising that if you can't win a game, you make sure you don't lose it. We could have seen this as one of those games and taken the replay but we wanted to win. We kept going for the winner. We just couldn't get that second goal and then they went and scored for the upset.

We lost 2-1. Out of the FA Cup in the third round against a non-league side. It felt like the whole world had opened up and we wanted to be swallowed up. We went into the changing rooms and everyone was sitting quietly. I just wanted to get home. I'll never forget, the manager came in and just said, 'Listen, I don't need to tell you anything boys. You'll read it all in the morning.' That was it. We got back to the Connexion, fans were there having a go at us, saying we weren't fit to wear the shirt. They were entitled to their say. The next day it was all over the papers. I didn't know what to do. I couldn't hide my face and not go out, everyone around knew me. I just wanted the next game to come as quickly as possible.

But it came back again when Sutton played in the fourth round and were beaten. It was all dragged up again and still gets dragged up every year now when it's the third round of the cup.

That's just the ups and downs of football. We weren't the first and we won't be the last to dominate a game but lose. There are bigger teams than us that have done that. At the time, though, it felt like the end of the world. We'd let down all those fans, the ones at the game and the ones at home. We should have done enough to win the game. We had about 24 efforts on goal and they had three, and the rest is history.

I continued my recovery from injury, and while I wouldn't say I went back at 100 per cent – no one can do that I was getting there. I know I'd have got there. I'd have got back to my best for Coventry City but then we come back to the word loyalty. I'd wanted the club to show me some loyalty with that four-year contract but it turned out that I was heading for the exit at Highfield Road.

10

From Wembley to Wednesday

MY TIME at Coventry came to an end in early 1989. The club had accepted a bid from Sheffield Wednesday and told me I could go and talk to them. I was hearing at Coventry that I wasn't going to be the player that I'd been and we had other players who'd come in, so they felt they could let me go. I had to think about my future and my family. Sheffield Wednesday were a big club and their manager Ron Atkinson had a certain panache about him with the way that he wanted to play, so I thought it could be the right move for me to go and push on.

Ron Atkinson:

> I think he was my first signing at Wednesday. We were looking for a right-sided player and I thought we had Gordon Strachan lined up to come in from Manchester United. But then at

the last minute Leeds United made him the highest-paid player in the country and that one went out of the window. We were looking around for alternatives because we'd just got rid of Mark Proctor to Middlesbrough. We understood that Dave was available so we went in for him. I had a word with Cyrille about him and Cyrille was complimentary about Dave. Obviously, I'd seen him play before and games like the cup final as well, so we went for him. He had good ability, good control, pace, could beat a man and cross the ball.

I can remember him playing for Manchester City when I was at West Brom at Maine Road. That was when he first caught my eye, right back then. When he came in for me at Sheffield Wednesday he did well. He was good in training, had a good personality and we needed somebody like that, we needed one or two players short-term. We were in a desperate position and he came in and did exactly the job that I wanted that season.

I was sad to leave. I didn't want to go but the way things were going at the club told me that I had to. My only regret is that the cup-winning side was split up too early. That team should have been broken up slowly over a couple of years. John Sillett was up there as the best manager I worked with, along with Malcolm Allison. John and I became personal friends because he liked racehorses. It didn't go down too well with me that he wanted to let me go. Because of our outside interests and mutual friends we'd still see each other at race meetings and say hello to each other. It took a while to repair our relationship. I was bitter about it. I just had to take it. But that team should have been kept together for longer. Within a couple of years a lot of that team had been sold. I could have stayed for longer, Cyrille had more to offer, so did Peakey, a lot of us did. I was still in my prime. I'd broken my leg but I had enough time in my career to get back to my best and push on even more.

Coventry had a lot of players come in and out after I left. What they needed was that one or two quality new additions each year to build on what we already had. It didn't work out like that, and then by 1990 John Sillett was sacked. They sacked him while he was ill on his sickbed, which was very disappointing. He'd helped us win the FA Cup and then led us to three top-ten finishes and ended up sacked. But then it all comes back to that word again: loyalty.

I was at Coventry one day and gone the next. I went and got my gear and cleared my locker and I was gone.

People were surprised I was going because I'd been there for so long, but that's where we were. We'd won the FA Cup and got no reward from the club. I wanted to go and better myself. I was part of that backbone of the side with Oggy, Peakey and Cyrille. I thought I'd have been rewarded for that but it didn't happen. That was sad. I have been recognised by the club in the years since I left. I'm very proud to have been inducted as one of the members of Coventry's Hall of Fame. I'm so proud to be part of the club's history. I was part of winning the biggest trophy that the club have ever won. It's nice to be remembered. I appreciate the fans for remembering me and I want them to know that the feeling they have for me, I've got the same feeling for them.

* * *

Anyway, that was me finished at Coventry, so I went and met Big Ron halfway down the motorway because he lived around Birmingham. I'm sure he'd have spoken to Cyrille, so Cyrille would have told him what I was like. We did the deal and that was it, I was a Sheffield Wednesday player. I spoke to Cyrille about Ron, and he told me what a character he was, and he definitely was that. I got there and they had some good players like Carlton Palmer, David Hirst, Dalian Atkinson, Roland Nilsson. We had a strong side but were struggling at the wrong end of the table and in danger of relegation. It was very different going in there. I came in on money that was on par with what I was earning at Coventry.

I got on well with Big Ron but I never got on with the coach, Richie Barker. He wanted me to do things that I wasn't used to doing. He had a different approach to what I had done at Coventry and I didn't agree with some of his methods and his approach to the way that he wanted me to play. We had a very off and on relationship but I was perfectly fine with Big Ron. Richie wanted me to close the full-back down in a different way to how I was used to. He wanted his back four to stay where they were. If the ball went to the winger I had to work from the full-back to get to the winger. I thought my full-back would close down the winger but Richie wanted the back four to be very rigid and stay in their shape. I used to think that if the full-back had the ball under control, he'd just pass it by me so I'd wait, but Richie wanted me to close him down as soon as possible and then when he passed to the winger he wanted me to get straight to the winger. I was doing a job where I thought my full-back could help me. I was wondering what was going on. If I closed the winger down and then we broke down the left-hand side, he'd want me to be up there on the right side supporting the attack. I was thinking, *Woah, hang on a minute!* At Coventry, the winger and full-back worked in tandem so if I closed the full-back and he passed to the winger, then my full-back would close down the winger. I disagreed with Richie on that.

On the training ground, Ron was a big character. He loved his five-a-sides; we'd always have a five-a-side. He'd say to me, 'Right, I'm going to go pick on someone today.' He'd choose someone to go pick on to get them going. He loved the 400 metres as well, and laps. He really loved the five-a-sides, though. He always picked himself for a five-a-side. First half, he'd play left wing and then he'd go right wing second half, so when he changed ends he just had to turn around! He wanted you to enjoy training but he'd work you hard. We'd often do five-mile runs. He'd give us the 400 metres as well, where you had to get to the front otherwise you'd have another 400 metres to do. He wasn't so big necessarily on tactics, he just wanted you to enjoy your football. He wanted you to be yourself on and off the pitch.

Sometimes a manager has to put their arm around you, sometimes they don't. Ron Atkinson didn't mind players going at each other at half-time. He wanted us to sort it out rather than leaving it all down to the manager. Ron was probably the one that stood out in that way that he didn't mind arguments and fisticuffs. I didn't like that. I thought if anyone was going to have a go at me it should be the manager because that was his job. With a manager like John Bond, sometimes the cups of tea could go flying. You'd know when you went into the changing room that you needed to be on your guard because you were about to get a telling-off. Len Ashurst was like that as well. They just wanted the best for the team and they'd get frustrated. With Ron, when someone in the changing room thought something was wrong, he wanted the players to sort it out rather than him doing it himself. Whether you were right or wrong, he liked that. I'd been brought up differently, so that was all new to me.

Soon after arriving, I found that players would have a go at each other in the changing room after a game. They'd be blaming each other, saying it was this person's fault and they should have done this or they lost their runner or whatever. Because of the years I'd had before in the changing rooms I'd been in, I came into that changing room and thought, *Ohhhh...* You take on board what people say to you in that kind of changing room. You dissect it, and if I thought it was unfair then I'd probably have a go on the Monday morning. By that time, the manager or the player who said it might have calmed down and changed their opinion. Sometimes, in a dressing room like that one at Sheffield Wednesday, people can go over the top and they realise it afterwards, and then you clear the air the next day. To go from the Coventry dressing room into that kind of atmosphere was strange to me. Big Ron didn't mind that kind of dressing room and players having a go at each other. I wasn't one for that.

Ron liked a little bit of socialising from the lads. He didn't like too much but if we were doing the business and winning then he'd be alright. Some days he'd lay the law down and be strict and say we couldn't go out, and the lads didn't like that. He used to take us to Oxford and the lads would be running for four or five days and he wouldn't give us any time to ourselves. The lads thought that was wrong. He was the type of manager where if you lost you knew about it. You'd be in the next day and he'd run you. If you won, you'd have the next day off. That's how he was.

Of course, Ron would years later get into trouble for a racist remark made while he was working for ITV. He thought he was off-air but his remark about Chelsea defender Marcel Desailly was picked up on some of the international broadcasts. I never had any problems with Ron and he liked black players playing for him, so that came as a big surprise to me. Some would say that he hadn't meant what he said, but sometimes people don't get a second chance. Some people can say things and say they didn't mean it. You can maybe get away with that as a young kid, but when you're older you know what you're saying. Trust me, you know what you're saying. As a young kid you might say things because you've heard your mum or your dad or your friends say it, but he wasn't a young kid, and when you're older you should know better.

I made my debut in a 2-0 defeat to QPR at Hillsborough. To be honest, that game doesn't stick out too much in my mind other than I wanted to go and make a good impression. Hillsborough had always been a good ground for me and that was one of the reasons why I moved there because I'd always liked playing there. I didn't pull up any trees really on my debut. We were in a difficult time and just wanted to stay up.

Not long after I joined came a terrible day: 15 April 1989 is a day that football fans will never forget. It was the FA Cup semi-final between Liverpool and Nottingham Forest at Hillsborough. As we all know, it was a terrible day in which a dreadful crush in the stadium led to 97 supporters losing their lives. For me it was particularly poignant. It happened at our home ground and had a massive impact on the city. I was watching the game at home on TV. I was injured at the time. I'd been there with Coventry two years before for the semi-final against Leeds when the fans couldn't get in and the decision was made to delay the kick-off by half an hour. I was watching and wondering why they hadn't delayed the kick-off. It was a disaster waiting to happen. It was awful watching it unfold on the TV. The following day I had to go into Hillsborough and, because I was a player, I was allowed through the gates. I wasn't allowed to touch anything in the ground but I could see the devastation that had happened just the day before. It was awful. It was unbelievable. People talk about what they saw that day on the pitch and it devastated the Sheffield Wednesday players because we saw the damage that had been done and this scene of devastation. There were parts of the ground that we weren't allowed to go into, including the gym. People were outside the ground giving me flowers to put down on the pitch.

It had a big impact on the players, just knowing what had happened in our own ground. It took a toll on the players. You couldn't escape it. People were talking about it everywhere and every day. We couldn't play at Hillsborough for a little while. It was something that we all knew about but we didn't really speak about it among the squad. It affected everyone in different ways. We had people in the club facing criminal charges, it affected the players, the background staff, everyone. It was a very weird atmosphere when we went back to play at Hillsborough for the first time after the disaster. We played West Ham on 9 May and the Leppings Lane end was covered in black tarpaulin. The whole rest of that season was weird. It was a very subdued day. When I speak to people now about the Hillsborough disaster, they don't realise the impact it had on some of the Sheffield Wednesday players. The first couple of games we played at Hillsborough after the disaster, a couple of players got injured. We had to get the pitch blessed. It affected us in all sorts of ways.

I made ten appearances in the run-in that season. That team shouldn't have been struggling at the bottom and we had enough to pull away to safety. We got some big wins in March and April, 3-1 against Newcastle and 3-0 over Millwall. We beat Middlesbrough 1-0 in the penultimate match of the season and then drew 2-2 with Norwich on the final day. That meant we finished three points above the relegation places, with Newcastle, West Ham and Middlesbrough the three that dropped down to the division below. That team shouldn't have been struggling and that was proven the next year because they went and did very well. John Sheridan came in, and I got on very well with him because he's from the same part of Manchester as me. He became a big cog in that team.

The following season I came back to Highfield Road for a league game with Sheffield Wednesday on 17 March 1990 and it almost brought a tear to my eye. The crowd gave me a standing ovation. That was how much the Coventry fans thought of me. That was so pleasing. It was a strange day to go back to Highfield Road but not playing for Coventry. We won 4-1 that day. The response from the Coventry crowd sat with me so well because I knew, no matter how much fans might dislike you sometimes, you still had all these thousands of people who wanted to give me that recognition. They recognised that I put in good service for the club. They recognised that I hadn't just been there for a year or two, I'd had six good years there and given my all for the club. To be remembered by the fans was enough for me.

With Sheffield Wednesday, we got to the League Cup Final in the second season but I left because I wanted to go and play football. That was my decision to leave. I could have stuck around and been a part of winning the League Cup but I just wanted to play football while I still had a lot to offer. I wasn't getting in the team as much and Coventry had tried a few wingers like Ray Woods and Dougie McGuire, and they didn't really fit in the jigsaw. After I'd met John Sillett a few times at the racing I was thinking of leaving Sheffield Wednesday because I wanted regular football and John was trying to get me back to Coventry. It was too late by that time, though, it just didn't quite work with the timings. Knowing that they wanted me back helped heal the bitterness that I had about the way I left the club. He brought in players who he thought were better than the players he was letting go, but they weren't. But John Sillett tried to get me back to Coventry, although I didn't know that at the time, and I ended up moving on from Sheffield Wednesday and signing for Swindon.

11

The End is Nigh

I WASN'T getting on with Barker, the Sheffield Wednesday coach, we'd disagreed and we all thought it would be best for us to part ways. I just wanted to play football. I became aware that Swindon wanted to take me during the season. I knew they were looking at me. The problem with Swindon was they'd just been done for some alleged offences. They won the play-offs at the end of the 1990/91 season but were kept in the Second Division because of these offences. I just wanted to go and play football. Being kept in the Second Division could have gone two ways. It could have knocked everyone or you could use it as motivation to make sure you go up the right way the following season. I wanted to be part of that and help the club go up automatically so we didn't need the play-offs.

Ossie Ardiles was manager at the time. His management style was typical of how he played the game. He wanted his

THE END IS NIGH

teams to get forward and be very attack-minded. You could see that a few years later when he was manager at Spurs. His attitude was that if we let four in it was okay as long as we scored five. He was a good manager and a good man. I was ready for a good season with Swindon but I had the worst possible start – I broke my leg in my second game for the club. It was a match against Darlington, Gary Gill came in with a tackle and I broke my tibia and fibula. He came in to make sure I didn't move away with the ball but I was too quick. He didn't come in meaning to break my leg but I think he came in to foul me. I knew straight away it was a bad one.

You don't get as many tackles like that today. The game is better in that way and players get more protection. It was the same leg that I'd broken at Coventry. It was hard to stomach because, other than the previous broken leg, I wasn't a player that was used to being out injured. All of a sudden, I was carrying these big injuries and that takes a toll on you physically and mentally. I was 31 and wondering if my career was finished. Would I ever get back to the player I'd been? Would I ever be the same mentally? It was a big injury to come back from but at the same time I still believed in myself. I thought I still had plenty of petrol in the tank. My thinking was even if I couldn't get back playing football at that level, I wanted to get back to playing somewhere at some level. That was just my love for the game. I wanted to still be an influence and carry on. I still had things to do. I wanted to get back to scoring goals and enjoying the good times after the bad times. I wanted to still be contributing to the game.

One way that I contributed while I was out injured was through scouting. When I broke my leg at Coventry, I had Lloydy, who was recovering at the same time. I didn't have that this time. While I was injured, Swindon changed the manager. That was massive because a new manager will look at you differently. Ossie left and Glenn Hoddle came in. The last game I'd played against Hoddle was the cup final so I don't think that went down too well with him. I was injured when he took over and we didn't see eye to eye at all. Me and Glenn never got on. You could say that his man-management wasn't the best. The less said about Glenn the better. We didn't get on and that was it.

I took on a scouting role at that time while I was getting back fit. Glenn gave me that role to watch the teams in the Midlands and report back to him. I'd write a report on teams that we were due to play, looking at how the teams played, the best way to break them down, their strengths and weaknesses. I enjoyed it. I saw scouting and coaching as something I could move into when I finished playing. I felt I had a lot to offer. I could help unpick how to beat teams and how to play against them. That was one good thing in a frustrating period of my career. I wasn't in a good place after breaking my leg again. I was ready to put in the work to get back though. But again it was there in the back of my mind whether my leg was weaker now. I'd broken it twice, would I break it again?

When I came back that was still in the back of my mind when I went in for tackles. It was tough physically and mentally. I needed good people around me and I needed to believe that I could get back to the level that I'd been at while I was with Coventry. You have to try to just stay focused when you're out with a long-term injury. Again, it was that thing of watching other players being signed to take my place. I was classed as being no good to the team because I was out for nine months. That's a whole season, so they had to replace me. That's hard when you're used to playing all the time. Things never got going for me at Swindon because of the injury and then my old manager from Manchester City, John Bond, took me to Shrewsbury on loan. I wanted to go there, get some games and get fit. I wasn't getting in the team at Swindon so I wanted to get out and keep fit. I wanted to prove that I could still play, to others and also to myself.

Unbelievably, in my second game for the club I broke the same leg again. We were playing Stockport and I'd scored twice in the game and was doing well. The manager of Stockport was a guy named John Sainty, who'd been John Bond's assistant at Man City. I was having a bit of a game and what I've heard is that he said they'd not laid a finger on me and they had to let me know they were there. He'd coached me at Man City and knew exactly what kind of player I was. Unfortunately, the lad let me know he was there a little bit more than he should have done and I ended up with yet another broken leg.

The only good thing was that I'd been through it before and I knew exactly what I had to do to get back fit again. But even then you don't know how it's going to set or any problems that you might have on the way. You get back and when you think you're fit you're still not fit, and the strength that you need isn't there. So many things went through my mind. I was wondering if I'd play again and, if I did, then who would I be playing for. What level would I be playing at? As always with me, I just wanted to play football. I just got on with it and dealt with it as best I could, even though I was wondering if I'd ever kick a ball again.

**

I got myself back fit and got back into the Swindon team for a pre-season match against Yeovil. I'd worked so hard to get back fit again and suffered yet another blow – yet another broken leg. I can't describe the feeling to break that same leg for the fourth time. Obviously, I thought there was a weakness there. I'll never be able to describe that feeling. I wouldn't wish it on anyone. I was devastated. That's the only word I can use. I was back in the same place yet again. So many things were going through my head. I had so much time on my hands while I was out to think about all these things and all the hurdles I had to go through to get back again. The medical people told me if I broke it again I'd have one leg shorter than the other. I'd rather do it on the football pitch, though, than some kind of accident like someone knocking a chair into me in the pub. There was a lot of anguish. I'd gone from the high life of being an FA Cup winner to breaking my leg on four separate occasions.

They were very frustrating times. I hadn't fulfilled my career potential and had to retire because of the broken legs. I still had plenty of petrol in the tank and the desire was still there. I wanted to pass my experience on as well to younger players. As I said, the decision to finish playing was out of my hands. Breaking the same leg four times means not many clubs are going to trust you. I still wanted to play, though, so I started to play semi-pro. When I went down to non-league, I always got a hostile reception from the opposition. The other side would always let me know they were there. There was still that little regime of racism in the game as well. I didn't get any favours, let's put it that way.

It was like the early days. I had to look after myself. I played for Nuneaton Borough, Atherstone Town and Hinckley Athletic. Obviously, the contract and money side of things was very different to my Coventry days, but money didn't come into it for me. As I've already said, I just wanted to play football. It was difficult playing at that level because I was a name. You didn't have many FA Cup winners at that level. I had to wear two pairs of shin pads. I was determined, though. I felt that I still had something to offer. Even if I wasn't playing, I could still pass my knowledge on to other players. I thought I could coach and help players. I wanted that role but not many black guys were getting the opportunities in coaching, so it was very difficult to get a foot on the ladder as a black guy. It wasn't a case of not being good enough, it was that there weren't many of us around. Racism played a part, I can't sit on the fence with that. As experienced as I was, I still needed doors to open, and not many doors were opening for black guys who wanted to get into coaching and management. We're talking 25 years ago and even now we still don't have enough black guys in management.

I enjoyed those days playing in non-league. It was good to see the other side of football, having played for so many years at the top of the pyramid. I've had a lot of adversity in my career from way back to my Manchester City days. I had racism to contend with and then the broken legs, and I think all that made me even more determined to keep on playing for as long as I could, even if it was at a lower level than I was used to. I never felt I was better than playing in the lower leagues. Eventually, I decided to retire and I felt something was around the corner for me in coaching. I was coaching while I was at Atherstone and felt I could get into coaching, but it was just very difficult to get my foot on the ladder.

I was trying to get that foot on the ladder and I couldn't get one. Very few black former players were getting jobs in coaching. That was very disappointing. It was a disaster to not get that chance. With the experience I had as a player and the managers I'd played under, you'd have thought that I'd have had a lot to offer as a manager or a coach. I'd done all my coaching badges and just wanted to get that opportunity, and it never happened. I had to look for something else. I tried for a long time for that opportunity. I wanted to help players come on. I did that bit of coaching at Atherstone and thought I could push on from there but it never developed. I'd have been happy to start at the bottom and work up because I was still learning. If that chance to be a manager had come, I'd have taken it in my stride, but it didn't happen. To this day I still want to give back to younger players and help young pros.

There's still not many black managers around today. There's a lot of managers, though, who can't speak a word of English who get jobs here. You don't see many English managers who can't speak Spanish getting jobs in Spain. It's a bit weird to me. The opportunities still aren't there for black managers. People like Paul Ince and Sol Campbell, who have captained England, had to go down to the lower leagues. It also seems that black managers get fewer chances if things don't go well in a job, then they're tarnished. We've just got to keep fighting for black managers and keep on knocking on the door.

Racism today in comparison to the 70s and 80s has come a long way. Even so, we still have cowards on social media who abuse and troll. As the game has developed, we have players coming from all different backgrounds and ethnicities. Things are getting better but racism will always be there. I don't think it will ever go away. The PFA are doing what they can about it but I still don't think they do enough. I do what I can but I'm not going to change the world in my lifetime. Things have changed today. Back when I was playing, I'd get racist abuse shouted at me from the terraces. I'd get abuse from players on the pitch. You could do something about it when someone abused you on the pitch. If someone abused you from the terraces you could maybe give them a hand signal or score a goal and shut them up. With social media, you can't do anything about it. People on social media say things that can destroy people, not just to black people but all races. They're destroying people from their phone or behind a computer. Still, things have got better compared to what I went through when I'd be walking down the street and people would be shouting abuse at me and I'd have to just walk away. People weren't hiding behind anything in those days, it was right there in your face.

When you're out, you're always going to get fans who like you and fans who don't like you. When you're winning, fans love you. Sometimes that could get too much when we were out and the fans would know where we were and would come over to us. It's part and parcel of football, though; if you're doing well you've got to expect that. I'd rather a fan come up to me and ask for a photo than someone coming up to me saying I'm shit! That can have a big impact on your social life and you can imagine what it does to your confidence. After a bad result, people might be unhappy to see you out but you might be out with your family for a meal that you'd arranged beforehand. People would still want to come and speak to you even if you were out with family. Even after a bad result I'd try to enjoy myself. If you've had a bad game you know better than anyone else, you don't need anyone else to tell you. If you've got any pride in yourself, then you know when you've had a bad game. You'll wake up the next day and the paper will tell you that you've had a bad day. Then you'll get into training and the manager will tell you that you'd had a bad day. You learn about yourself in times like that and you learn if you've got some balls about you. We all have bad days, it's about how you deal with them and how you learn from them, how you fix them and how you make sure it doesn't happen again.

Today, the players take abuse on social media but they also get so many accolades. If you choose to be on social media then you've got to take the good with the bad. People will troll you because they think they can get away with it. I completely disagree with that because it can destroy someone and their confidence. I'm not on social media because of that. I wouldn't have been on social media if they'd had it when I was playing. I wouldn't want all the praise on social media that comes from scoring the winning goal in a game because there's also all the nasty things that are said about you.

As well as social media, another thing that has changed since I played is that the balls are different, the pitches are better so you can pass the ball a lot quicker. I believe some of the players I played with could play today and some of the players who play today couldn't have played when I played because it was so much more physical back then. Tactics and coaching have changed but it's still the same game, you've still got to get that ball in the back of the net.

Keith Houchen says on this subject:

> Dave was a fantastic player. The way that the game's played now would suit him down to the ground, he would flourish in today's game. The likes of me, big Cyrille and Killer might have had to adapt a bit more!

Oggy agrees:

> If you ask me to sum up Dave I would say he was a big-game player. He was outstanding in the big games. People talk about the cup final but generally in all the big games he would show his talent. Sometimes people focus on the cup final and forget about the other big-game performances that he put in.
>
> You have to remember, he started off at Manchester City and played big games there as well. He was a footballer who was very pleasing on the eye. He could drift past players and go

either way and he didn't just rely on pure pace, he had much more to his game. He was versatile, he could play out wide as he often did, where he could take players on and show his skill, or he could play down the middle.

In today's game he would absolutely thrive as a No.10 or in a front three. The modern game wouldn't suit every player from back then but Dave would have been absolutely made for it. When you think about the billiard table pitches that they play on now and the light balls, the fact that the opposition can't be as physical as they used to be – the modern game would have suited him even more than back when he played. He would be a big star at today's level as well as back then. Back then at Coventry, we were a very disciplined, well-organised side and we were creative with the ball, but when out of possession we had to defend, and Dave knew how to defend. He would double up with the full-back when he was playing wide right. He was a very clever player and knew how to track runners and how to detach himself and attack when we had possession.

Football today would suit me down to the ground. Today, if a guy puts in one tackle on you he's likely to get a yellow card. In my day, the referee would let the defender have one free tackle on you. I think I'd do very well if I played today. Still, I did alright for myself as a top-flight regular for years and an FA Cup winner. Not bad for the 'little coloured boy', right?